Designing in Batik and Tie Dye

Designing in Batik and Tie Dye

Nancy Belfer, ASSOCIATE PROFESSOR OF TEXTILE DESIGN

STATE UNIVERSITY COLLEGE at BUFFALO, NEW YORK

Davis Publications, Inc.
WORCESTER, MASSACHUSETTS

Copyright© 1972
Davis Publications, Inc.
Worcester, Massachusetts, U.S.A.

Library of Congress Catalog Card Number: 72-185461
ISBN: 0-87192-047-6

Printing: Davis Press, Inc.
Type: IBM Selectric Theme and Univers,
    set by Anco Technical Services, Inc.
Design: Jane Pitts

10 9 8 7 6 5 4 3

Contents

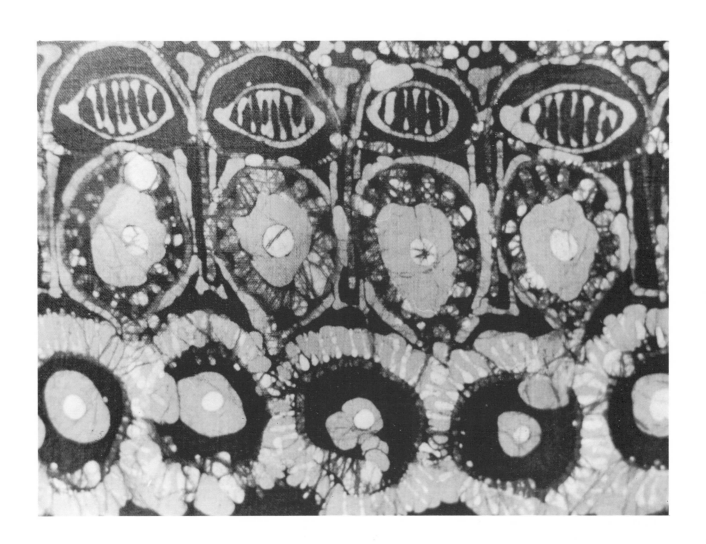

Introduction

There are a few links with the ancient past that have not been completely rejected by our immersion in the daily marvels of a mechanized age. These links seem worth caring about and continuing. In different times and in different parts of the world, ideas evolved about using coloring agents. These, together with various other materials, were applied in a manner that formed a protection or "resist" on the cloth. The sections of the cloth so protected would not be colored by the dye; when the resist material was removed, the image emerged.

The hand embellishment of textiles with natural colorants, or dyes, was known to the most primitive of peoples. The resist techniques, requiring the methods of tying, folding, binding of the cloth, as well as the application of penetrating starch pastes or hot wax solutions, were known before the beginnings of recorded history. The uses of dyes and mastery of dye technology are considered by some scholars to be among the more significant achievements of civilized man. In some areas, these skills developed with astonishing sophistication; and then, as religious, political, economic or cultural changes occurred, long-used knowledge became lost.

Many of these processes have been kept alive and today are revitalized by contemporary attitudes about expressive values in art. The traditional examples illustrated in this book give eloquent testimony to the careful complexity of the design motifs as well as the richness of the dye coloration. These pieces are not meant to serve as models to be imitated. They are presented as utilitarian design solutions coming from a particular culture at a particular time, with the symbolic patterning and imagery reflecting very specialized needs and values. We can learn much by studying these pieces, with the realization that today fine skills are most relevant when they allow the artist to pursue his own inventive spirit.

This book describes the historical applications of batik and tie dye resist techniques, as well as a wide range of contemporary approaches and innovations. It is a book for those who wish to learn skills, which are certainly necessary and important. But it is also for those who wish to encourage their ability to see beyond the obvious, to struggle beyond the commonplace. Work in these resist-dye textile processes can offer a fascinating challenge, a creative experience of deep pleasure and accomplishment.

N. B.

Shapes of hearts and dots alternate on a modern batik cloth, made in Turkey. Black dye on red fabric.

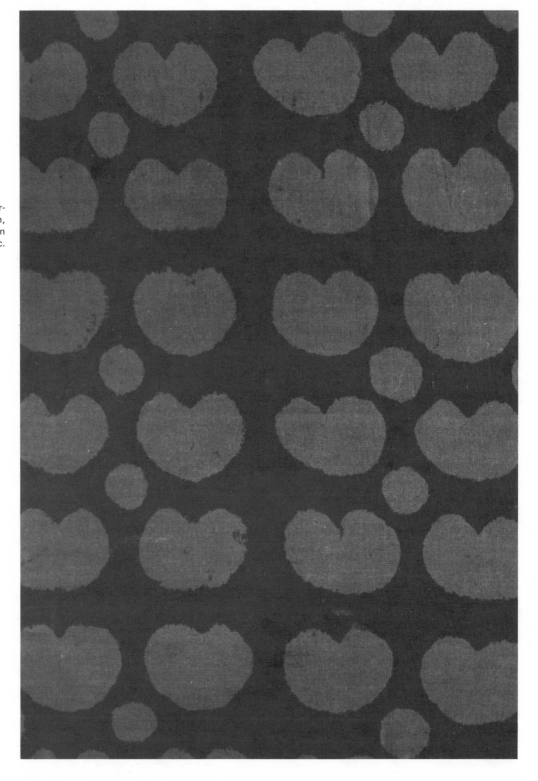

Early Uses of Dyes

Dyes are a kind of magic, a delight to the eye and a joy to use. Even a brief inquiry into the early discoveries and uses of these coloring agents conveys a sense of mystery and glamour. Primitive people in many different parts of the world discovered that certain root, leaf or bark material could be treated to produce color in a fluid form. Its application was both religious and functional—the embellishment of body, clothing and utensils.

Ancient Chinese writings, 2,500 B.C., mention the use of dyes on cloth. The Peruvians, during a time corresponding to the first centuries of the Christian era, worked with well over a hundred distinct hues in their textiles. The superb mastery of dyeing skills which developed in India was praised throughout the Roman world; excavated cloth fragments indicate a tradition going back some 5,000 years.

A close look on a fanciful insect; one of many on a traditional Javanese batik sarong.

In Greek antiquity, myths often allude to dye colorings. Of intriguing interest is one of the few truly fast dyes in use at this time: purpura, extracted from gland secretions of mollusks along the Greek coastline. It was known to the Phoenicians and has been traced back to Minoan Crete. The term "purple" was applied to the range of red to blue violets made from these shellfish secretions, a colorless liquid which oxidized when exposed to air. Hills of crushed shells today identify the remains of extensive dye works. The color was difficult to process and was used only to dye the finest garments, robes and cloaks worn throughout the Mediterranean world as a distinctive mark of luxury.

Purple has since become a symbol of aristocratic pomp and celebrity, the color of royalty. Strangely enough, knowledge of this color, known as Tyrian purple, became lost during the Dark Ages. It was rediscovered by a French scholar in the middle of the nineteenth century, about the same time chemically made dyes were first introduced in England.

Numerous plants, certain insects and shellfish, as well as some minerals, have been found to be sources of colorants. Knowledge of the preparation and usage of natural dyes evolved slowly over centuries of trial and error experimentation. The formulas and recipes were often carefully protected secrets, subject to cloak and dagger intrigues and trade conflicts among rival countries. In India, where resist dyeing probably originated, the complex technology involved in the formulation of dyes and mordants was mastered to an unparalleled degree of perfection. Indian textiles were known and prized by Europeans since the sixteenth century.

In the resist-dye techniques, the dyeing of the cloth cannot be thought of as the application of pigment to surface; there must be a chemical reaction between the coloring agent and the fiber so that the color becomes a permanent, integral part of the fabric. In order to achieve this affinity between dye and cloth, and also to insure fastness and color control, the use of a mordant became necessary.

Mordants are chemical solutions which can be used before, during or after the dye bath, thus preparing the fiber to receive the color and also to control the actual hue obtained. The same dye used with different mordants will produce different colors. Some commonly used mordant substances are organic acids (acetic, tartar, tannic), inorganic acids (sulphuric), and salts (alum, tartar emetic, Glaubers salt). If a certain color is to be duplicated, the preparation of the dye solution as well as the mordant must be exactly the same.

Some of the oldest and most widely known of the natural dyes are:

Indigo — probably first used in India but known throughout East Asia before recorded history. This dye produces the familiar deep blue color so prevalent on Javanese batiks.

Madder — also originated in India; deep, rich reds are produced from powder formed by grinding the roots of the madder plant.

Cochineal — a range of brilliant reds; the grains are prepared from a dried insect, cocus cacti. This dye was first known in South America and Mexico.

2

Remarkably detailed, this section of a Javanese batik sarong pictures a proud bird in a garden of freely drawn flowers.

From here the list can be greatly expanded to include numerous additional plants as well as several species of insects, shellfish, minerals and metals. There is much interest today in the preparation of natural dyes. Excellent books are available which provide reliable directions for making and using the dyes and mordants. The raw materials can usually be collected personally or purchased from chemical supply firms.

A batik from India, this silk head scarf is in brilliant yellow and red, with stems and leaves in a smoothly flowing surface pattern.

Synthetic Dyes

Although it is only slightly over a hundred years ago that man-made dye substances were discovered, and even less time since they have become widely available, they have almost entirely replaced natural dyes. Except in some of the most remote areas of the world, techniques of dyeing with natural substances, perfected over many centuries, suddenly became obsolete. The reasons for this are easy to understand; the advantages of synthetic dyes, in terms of cost, brilliance and range of color, ease of handling and use, and fastness, cannot be denied.

During the early part of the eighteenth century, the first tentative experiments were made in the attempt to produce artificial dyes. From about 1850-1890, however, a series of discoveries in England and Germany resulted in rapid progress in dye chemistry. The first "aniline" dye colors were produced by synthesizing coal tar, a waste substance in the manufacture of gas. Among the earliest discoveries was alizarin crimson, a chemical duplication of the colorative material found in the madder root. Many additional colors were discovered during this time, and specialized classes or groups of dyes evolved. Even indigo, the most widely used natural dye, was produced synthetically by the beginning of the twentieth century.

Synthetic dyes do not, in most cases, require mordants, as they fuse directly to the fiber molecule without prior chemical preparation. Various salts and acids are used to assist in the dyeing procedure; temperature and rate of heating are also important factors.

Different classifications of dyes have an affinity for specific fibers. Cotton, linen, jute and viscose rayon are termed vegetable or cellulostic fibers. The class of direct dyes are most suitable. Wool and silk are protein or animal fibers, requiring acid dyes. Both direct and acid dyes can be used successfully with studio or home equipment. Other classes of dyes which can be adapted for individual use are basic, vat, and Procion.[TM] There are numerous other types of dyes manufactured, but their use is too complex or too technical for the individual craftsman; they are best suited to commercial application.

In regard to the use of these dyes, one additional point should be mentioned since only synthetic dyes are discussed in the technical section of this book. Often, when reading accounts of dyes and their application prior to the widespread acceptance of chemical dyes, one notices an obvious lament for a kind of beauty and softness found only in natural dyes. It is implied that natural dyes are somehow superior; synthetic dyes are called garish and lacking in warmth. This attitude appears frequently but seems to be based more on a kind of misapplied sentimentality rather than on a sound knowledge of dyes and dyeing procedures.

The most elementary understanding of color theory and dye usage should clarify this point. By increasing or decreasing the proportion of the dye used, and by intermixing the dye colors, any hue, tint, or shade tonality can be achieved. When synthetic dyes are used properly the colors have great richness and warmth, as well as a much higher degree of fastness than natural dyes. In addition, synthetic or aniline dyes are easy to obtain and are relatively inexpensive.

Resist dyeing from India, 18th century. The design on this detail from a horizontal panel is of Hindu origin. In a series of religious scenes from the life of Vishnu, the various deities parade before him, playing music.

The Resist Dye Processes in Textiles

The various types of resist dye processes can be best defined according to the type of resist which is used and the manner of its application.

Hot Wax Resist. A technique of imparting images on cloth requiring the application of hot wax to form a protective resist. The unwaxed sections of the fabric are then colored by the dye; the parts of the cloth containing the wax remain free of the dye. This process is known as batik throughout Indonesia, India and Japan.

Starch Paste Resist. The use of soluble flour pastes which are applied to the cloth and allowed to dry, thus forming a resist to the dye. This technique was known throughout Asia, but is especially identified with the textiles of Africa. In Nigeria, the term, ADIRE ELEKO, refers to indigo dyed fabric made in the starch resist method.

Tie Dye. The use of various folding methods which, together with tying and binding techniques, form the resist. These processes are known as PLANGI (Indonesia), BHANDHANA (India), ADIRE ELESO (Nigeria), and SHIBORI (Japan).

Tritik. The use of simple stitches sewn into the cloth. When the stitches are pulled tightly or gathered, the resist is formed. Tritik is an Indonesian term, but has been adopted by various cultures to identify this method of resist dyeing.

Clamping Methods. The use of solid flat objects or templates clamped around the fabric to form the resist. This is a variation of an ancient Japanese technique.

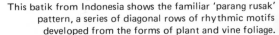

This batik from Indonesia shows the familiar 'parang rusak' pattern, a series of diagonal rows of rhythmic motifs developed from the forms of plant and vine foliage.

History and Tradition in Batik

Where does batik come from? There is no certainty, but several theories speculate on the origins of this intriguing craft. The word "batik" is Indonesian in origin, but the concept itself was probably first devised either by the Egyptians or, according to other scholars, on the Indian archipelago. It is known that liquid or paste starch resists preceded the use of wax.

In the fourth century B.C., the Greeks invaded India and returned with many textiles. This indicated an already well-established tradition in weaving, as well as cloth painting and dyeing. The images were geometric or highly stylized arrangements of flowers, fruits, birds and animals; the craftsmanship was of the highest quality. With increasing migration of people and expanding trade routes, knowledge of wax resist dyeing spread throughout Asia.

About 300 or 400 A.D. Indian traders and merchants introduced the technique to the Javanese peoples of Indonesia, who developed it in their own unique manner to the very high degree of excellence so admired today. Since the textile arts were of great importance to these people, the batiks of Indonesia give us an unusually complete and unbroken tradition that can be traced for centuries.

A section of a "slendang", a long, narrow strip of cloth worn as a shawl or scarf. The strong linear quality in the diagonal rows is obtained by scratching through the surface of the wax prior to dyeing.

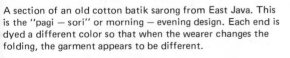

A section of an old cotton batik sarong from East Java. This is the "pagi — sori" or morning — evening design. Each end is dyed a different color so that when the wearer changes the folding, the garment appears to be different.

A "slendang" or cotton batik scarf cloth with a geometric border design and an unpatterned center.

The volcanic island of Java, where the batik art was perfected, was invaded by Hindu tribes from India who remained and were powerful rulers for 1300 years. During the Medieval period, Arabs came, also by way of India, introducing the Moslem religion. The sultans of these empires were supreme rulers with elaborate palaces and numerous court attendants; they lived storybook lives of richness and splendor. The usual preference for finery throughout Asia is for silk, but the Javanese, because of their ancient batik tradition, favored cotton. Cotton was easy to grow and in a tropical climate, a comfortable fabric to wear. Batik decoration was used only on garments, rather than ceremonial cloths or decorative hangings. At one time a sultan decreed that batik-making was a "royal art" to be practiced only by the women of the court. This ruling, of course, could not be enforced for long; the craft was too deeply ingrained among the people, but it serves as evidence of the value and high regard given these garments.

For centuries batik was practiced by the native villagers with a precision and concern for detail that we marvel at today. Time was of no importance; they employed infinite patience, working and reworking motifs

A Javanese woman working on a batik cloth with the tjanting tool.

A section of a cotton batik sarong from Java in the traditional allover pattern of triangular shapes, each embellished with a different motif.

handed down from one generation to another. A Dutch anthropologist, traveling through Java thirty years ago, gives an account of some of these native village practices:

"...I enjoy a visit to a village. There the meek woman sits quietly on a self-woven mat on the ground before the bamboo frame over which the white cotton is hanging loosely. On her back, tied in a 'slendang', a baby lies asleep; other children are crawling or running about the house; chickens everywhere—this is a humble house.

At her left is the earthenware little stove, the anglo, on which the charcoals melt some beeswax in a small iron vessel. She dips the tjanting, her only instrument into the liquid wax, blows then onto its thin outlet... and finally starts to make her design on the thin cotton. No pattern, no sketches on the cotton—her heart and imagination figure design the batik."*

The women were responsible for the designs and the waxing; the men, for the dyeing and finishing. The ingrained superstitions of many centuries played their part in the ritual of batik work. These skills were thought of as benevolent gifts from the spirits of ancestors. Good work was done only on a "good" day with tools that were blessed. Offerings of incense, rice and flowers were prepared to win the favor of the spirits. While the waxing demanded great skill, the dyeing procedures were extremely complicated and time-consuming; a slight error in mixing could prove ruinous. If the color was faulty, the evil spirits were surely at work.

*Adam, Tassilo, *The Art of Batik in Java*, Knickerbocker Weekly, August 28, 1944.

14

All of the traditional patterns had whimsical names—"a carefree life" or "moonshine charm"—which assist in identification. Certain patterns were reserved exclusively for the family of the sultan and his highest ranking officers. These were forbidden for use on other garments. The workmanship and dye coloration had to be perfect; this meant no sign of wax crackle, for any break in the wax meant faulty handling. Batiks with such "defects" had to be destroyed so that the evil spirits would not molest the ruler.

Some aspects of batik-making changed when the "tjap", or copper hand stamp, came into use in Java about 100 years ago. It was known in other areas for centuries. After the stamp is dipped into a bed of molten wax, the design motif is imprinted onto the cloth. The principle is that of block printing, with the hot wax taking the place of the ink. The stamp was made by inserting the edges of thin strips of copper into a wood base, conforming to a preplanned design. A second stamp was made of the reverse of each motif for printing on the back of the cloth.

This device has obviously made it possible for a batik to be completed in far less time than the tjanting method requires. The stamp, which so greatly speeded up the process, marked the beginning of the movement to change batik-making from a folk craft or "cottage industry" kind of activity to the small factory type of production that is prevalent today. There are several thousand of these factories in Java today. With some exceptions, aniline dyes have almost completely supplanted natural colorants. The last generation has seen many changes in the social structure which have added to the breaking down of the hand-craft traditions that existed, unchanged, for so many centuries.

A very old but intricately detailed "tjap" or stamping tool.

A Javanese batik worker printing a border design using the "tjap" tool.

A portion of an old batik scarf cloth patterned
in a profusion of birds, crabs and sea urchins.

To the Western eye, the design character of Javanese batiks seem to be
bound to a precise scheme of geometric repetition. Although some designs
seem more rhythmic than others, there is a lack of dramatic interplay of
the motifs. In the culture of these peoples, tradition was very strong—in
fact so strong that any deviation from ritual was a moral offense. This
attitude was bound to have its effect on the designs of the textiles. The
artist as a unique personality was simply of no concern, especially as batik
was a folk art, practiced among the villages. There was never a thought of
changing intentionally the basic scheme of a design as it was passed from
one generation to the next in a particular locality. These batiks should be
viewed today on the basis of strong cultural traditions.

Detail of design on preceding page.

Summary of Traditional Javanese Batik Method

1. Preparation of the cloth
   washed in hot water
   soaked in solution of castor oil or coconut oil
   oil boiled away
   cloth dried in sun
   placed in starch solution
   again dried in sun
   cloth pounded and beaten with wooden hammer

2. Application of the wax
   design drawn on the cloth
   tjanting tool—used to apply wax to outlines and linear motifs
   penembok—tool with a flat, wide spout, used for filling in larger sections
   tjap—a hand stamp, allowing the motif to be printed on the cloth
   (wax always applied to both sides of the cloth)

3. Dyeing the cloth
   cloth placed in indigo vat until the correct shade of blue is obtained (several days)
   fabric rinsed and dried
   wax scratched away from sections of the cloth which are to be dyed the next color (e.g. brown)
   additional wax applied to the sections which are to remain the indigo blue shade
   cloth dyed in the brown dye bath
   cloth rinsed and dried
   (some sections of the cloth will be blue, others brown; where the brown covers the unwaxed areas of blue, the resultant color is black)

4. Removing the wax
   fabric boiled in water to remove wax

A detail of the ''double-wing'' motif, one of the patterns
reserved for use by members of the royal court. This cloth
is a 40'' x 40'' head square, worn by men.

The border of a "slendang" shawl. The triangular or "tumpal"
shapes in the design are indigenous to Indonesia.

20

Indonesian puppet. The head, hands and torso are of carved
wood with the features painted in brilliant colors. The skirt
is made from a cotton batik cloth.

Section of a sarong
with a detailed design
of birds and flowers.

22

Dragon and exotic fish in a section of a cotton batik head
square from Indonesia.

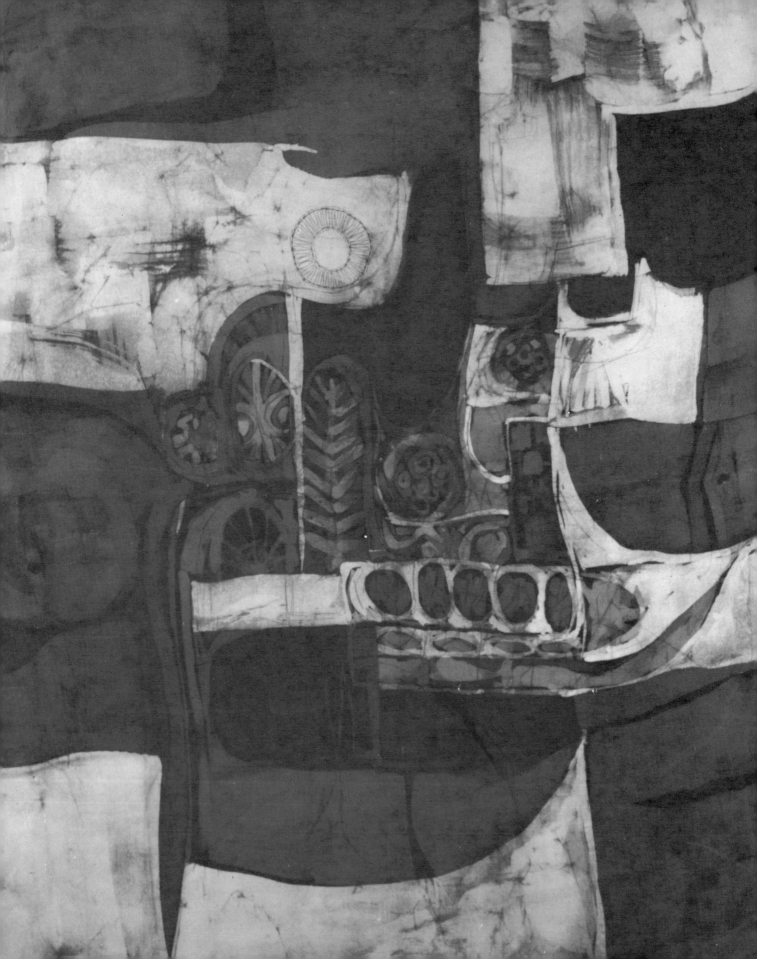

Contemporary Design in Batik

There are certain fairly precise procedural steps involved in the making of a batik. This does not imply, however, that there is a set of mechanical rules to be mastered which, if followed consistently, lead to ever predictable results. Working within a few basic guidelines, the "how" of making a batik becomes a fluid, personal means of expression. Certainly the nature of the technique is a fundamental aspect of those expressive qualities, but there are opportunities for an unusually wide range of graphic and color effects. Batik is a technique most responsive to the uniqueness of the individual temperament.

As the craftsman becomes proficient in handling the waxes, tools and dyes, he gains instinctive knowledge of the variety of visual effects possible. Along with this increasing technical competence, he develops an increasing sense of judgment in building color and form relationships. As in any creative media, mastery of the technical aspects is very much related to the qualitative concerns which often seem so elusive. Because of this, improvisation is suggested for the beginner as the most compatible means of allowing a personal imagery to unfold.

The very nature of the batik technique permits a fluid linear quality, as well as the solid shape structures possible when a wide brush is used to apply the wax. With dyeing and subsequent over-dyeing, a rich coloration is built that is often reminiscent of the transparencies found in stained glass windows.

ntrance View. Batik on cotton, 54″ x 42″. A contemporary
laptation of the ancient batik technique. In the large
apes, the hot wax was applied with a housepainting brush,
′ wide. Dyes were applied in both brush and dye bath methods.

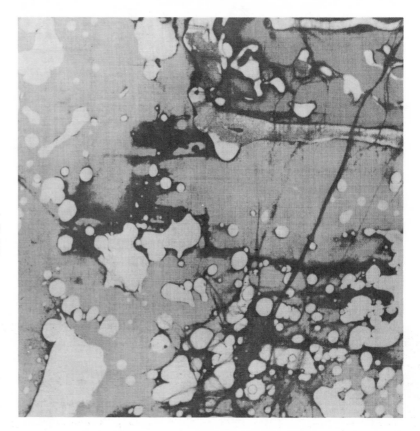

A beginning student applies wax to the cloth in a spontaneous manner, allowing it to drip on the fabric, forming
small, irregular shapes as seen in these designs.
(Gail Krakauer)

It is important to work in a medium long enough to gain real control in
handling it and to understand, through experience, some of its inherent
visual qualities. Creative thinking and planning seem to depend on an
interaction between this deep knowledge of the material and the kinds of
expressive ideas that can be formed by the artist. The more one works,
the stronger the grasp of this interaction. When the technical aspects of
batik have been understood, they become intuitive, almost automatic; the
expressive potential of the medium is then most fully realized.

For example, the line of wax made by a tjanting tool has a very different
quality from the line made by a brush; the line made by the small pointed
brush will be different from the line made by the wider, flat brush. The
character and uniqueness of these different kinds of lines are brought into
focus by the craftsman, as he masters the use of his tools. When he fully
understands what the tools can do, he can use them to best advantage.

While line and shape are the elements first considered in batik, it is color
that becomes the most forceful visual aspect of the work. There are many
theories about color usage which can be studied; some are very basic,
others more complex. A basic knowledge of color terminology is helpful,
but effective color planning does not depend on rules.

With some experience, each individual can formulate color harmonies which are personally expressive and do not depend on a predetermined application of scientific theories. There are many factors which cause a color to change visually in relation to other colors used. Therefore, predictable color schemes, when applied to dye usage, can be confusing as well as confining.

Probably the best way for one to begin is by using the colors one prefers by temperament, with the realization that constant and continuous observation and evaluation are necessary. The usual manner of using the dyes in baths is from lighter to darker values. The overall effect is richly unified, since each new dye color intermixes with the previous hue. In direct brush methods, there is greater initial choice of color; the overall effect is bold, full of vibrant contrasts. Here again, with experience, the craftsman evolves his own manner of working, adapting the technique to his own personal requirements.

The batik technique is utilized in many aspects of contemporary creative endeavor. It is found in large murals, permanently installed in buildings; in wall hangings, mounted or framed; divider panels; casement hangings; and as a distinctive embellishment to clothing and a wide range of useful objects. Visually, the effects range from a dramatic personal statement to a rhythmic pattern surface.

For the beginner, the guiding aim is to learn by personal discovery, realizing the uniqueness of one's own way of achieving particular effects, and having the courage to experiment, to try out new ideas. On this basis, serious involvement in the batik process can become an experience of continuing artistic growth and technical confidence.

In this section of a wall divider panel, the familiar dots and lines of the tjanting tool are evident in the light areas. Subsequent dye baths were in yellow, orange, and brown. (Lee Tetkowski)

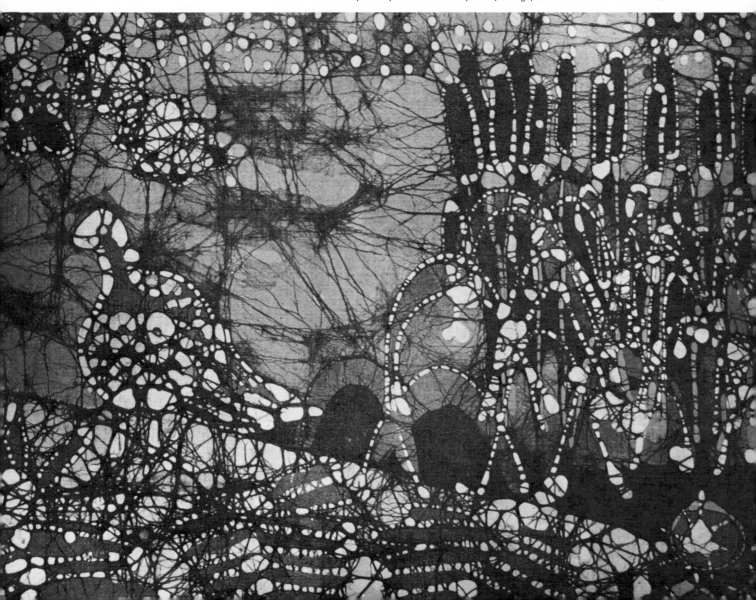

Preliminary Drawing and Sketching

Opinions will vary among artists working in batik as to the amount of preliminary planning that is necessary. Some feel that thorough planning is essential, with every aspect of the waxing and dyeing carefully worked out on paper beforehand. Others are more inclined toward an approach which allows for a certain amount of freedom to make decisions while the work is in progress. A certain amount of preliminary thinking is always necessary, but a complete colored "sketch" can be very restricting if used as a model to be duplicated in the batik process.

Certainly, an involvement with drawing, painting or collage-making can develop a personal sense of imagery that is essential to creative work in any media. In batik, line and shape formations are the initial design elements considered. Because of this, the quality of the drawing is important even though the medium is melted wax rather than ink, and the tool a tjanting or brush, rather than a pen. To think of lines of wax brushed or drawn on the cloth as merely a means of outlining a carefully sketched-in shape is to deny a wonderful vitality and flow of line. The initial application of the wax can convey a sense of spontaneity, of directness and immediacy; this is what gives contemporary batik a far different quality from the sometimes static design effects of traditional pieces.

Sketches are probably most valuable when they are used to give the artist a direction, clarifying the essentials of the idea and providing guidance for specific decisions during the development of the piece. The amount of planning can vary with the temperament and work habits of the artist. It can range from a fairly comprehensive color sketch, to an indication of line and tone, to a brief line drawing, to complete improvisation, working directly on the cloth with the brush or tjanting tool.

The most convenient method of transferring the sketch to the cloth is by drawing directly on the fabric with a stick of soft charcoal. If applied lightly, the charcoal will wash out in the dyes; pastel sticks, however, will leave a permanent mark and should not be used. Working in a freehand manner, the artist can quickly indicate the important aspects of the design, with complex details and variations incorporated as the piece develops.

If a more precise outline is required, as for a geometric design or a pattern calling for an exact repeat of the motif, the paper sketch should be drawn to the actual size of the fabric. The lines can be transferred by using carbon paper. This is best done on a sturdy table since pressure is necessary to go through the carbon paper on to the cloth. If large size carbon paper is not available, the standard smaller sheets can be lightly taped together.

Another method of transferring the sketch is by using a light box. This can be improvised by mounting a piece of plate glass or sheet of clear plastic over a light source. The drawing is placed on the glass, and over it the cloth; with the light coming through to the cloth the sketch can easily be seen and lightly traced with charcoal.

Some craftsmen prefer to use a tracing wheel which makes small perforations in the paper sketch. The paper, with these tiny holes outlining the design, is placed over the fabric. When charcoal or light colored chalk is dusted over the perforations, the lines of the design appear on the cloth.

Regardless of the transfer method used, the initial sketch should be thought of as a guide, providing direction and perhaps inspiration, rather than a finalized concept. There are unexpected surprises in the batik process; new ideas, new possibilities should be allowed and encouraged.

The Studio: Equipment and Supplies

Very little equipment is needed for batik work, and a small portion of a room can easily be adapted into a satisfactory studio arrangement. A sink or washtub should be in or nearby the work area. In addition, it is necessary to have:

1. Equipment
   a means of heating the wax—an electric fry pan, a glue pot,
       or a hot plate with double boiler arrangement
   a sturdy work table
   a wooden frame on which to stretch the cloth

2. Supplies and materials
   cloth
   wax
   dyes
   cleaning fluid

3. Small tools
   assorted brushes
   tjanting tool
   stamps for applying wax (optional)

4. Additional equipment
   large enamel pans for dye baths
   large, deep pot for steaming
   wide-top jars with covers
   stainless steel or plastic spoons
   rubber gloves
   thermometer
   measuring spoons
   electric iron
   plastic bags and sheet plastic
   newspapers

When using a photograph as the basis of a batik design, it becomes necessary to adapt the forms to the unique qualities of the wax and dye medium. Many directions are possible, evolving toward a strong structural simplicity or a complex interrelation of lines, shapes, and colors. (Lauren Belfer)

Summary of Contemporary Methods in Batik

The outlines which follow describe, in sequence, three different methods of working in the batik technique. Each procedure has its own unique visual qualities, reflected in the final result. The differences occur primarily in variations in the application of the dyes.

A detailed series of technical notes (see page 35) describe more completely the specific kinds of information necessary for a thorough understanding of the procedures involved.

Using the tjanting tool to apply the wax a young student built a rhythmic surface arrangement of lines, dots and simple shapes.
(Neil Tetkowski)

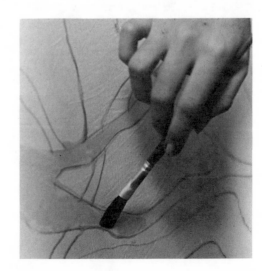

32

3

Method #1 (closest to traditional method)

1. Stretch prepared fabric on frame.
2. Sketch with soft charcoal.
3. Apply wax to areas retaining the color of the cloth.
4. Place the cloth in dye bath of first color for appropriate time, rinse, dry.
5. Attach fabric to frame.
6. Apply wax to areas that are to retain the first color.
7. Place the cloth in dye bath of second color for appropriate length of time, rinse, dry.

Steps 5., 6., and 7., can be repeated several more times.

8. If a crackle is desired, crush the cloth prior to the last dye bath. This is usually a dark color. Rinse, and dry.
9. Remove the wax, fix the dyes, and finish.

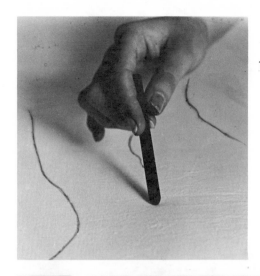

Method #2 (direct brushing of the dyes)

1. Stretch prepared fabric on frame.
2. Sketch with soft charcoal.
3. Apply the wax in areas retaining the color of the cloth. The design should be planned with self-contained shapes or islands of cloth surrounded by wax.
4. Brush the dyes directly onto the cloth, using different colors in the various shapes.
5. Allow time for the dyes to dry thoroughly.
6. Apply additional wax, introducing new shapes or motifs into the previously dyed sections.

Repeat steps 4., 5., and 6., or

7. Crush the cloth if a crackle effect is wanted, and place the cloth in a prepared dye bath. Rinse, and dry.
8. Remove the wax, fix the dyes, and finish.

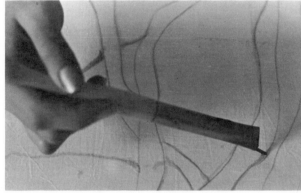

1. Sketching on the stretched cloth with charcoal.

2. Applying the wax with the tjanting tool.

3. Using a brush to apply the dye between previously drawn lines of wax.

4. Dyes of different colors are brushed onto the cloth, each shape enclosed by lines of wax.

5. When the dyes have dried, additional wax is applied with a brush.

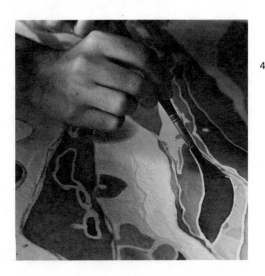

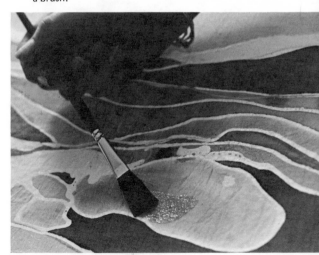

Method #3 (applying the dyes prior to waxing)

1. Stretch prepared fabric on frame.
2. Sketch with soft charcoal. (optional)
3. Using concentrated dye solutions, apply the color directly to the fabric. Brushes or small sponges can be used. The color will spread; sharp outlines will not be retained. Or, you may apply the color to the cloth using dye paste solutions which are easier to control than the liquids. Brushes of different sizes and sponges are satisfactory. The entire cloth area need not be covered with color.
4. Allow the dyes or dye pastes to dry thoroughly.
5. Using brushes and the tjanting tool, apply wax to the areas of color, as well as the background, defining the shapes and organizing the relationships between the dyed and undyed areas of the cloth.

Steps 3., 4., and 5., can be repeated, or,

6. If crackle is wanted, crush the cloth, and immerse in the last dye bath color for the appropriate time. Rinse, and dry.
7. Remove the wax, fix the dyes, and finish.

6. The cloth is lightly crushed to obtain a crackle effect.

7. The cloth is placed into the dye bath.

8. Following the dye bath, the waxed cloth is allowed to dry.

9. Removing the wax by ironing the cloth between sheets of newspaper.

10. The finished batik.

(demonstration by Lucille Licata)

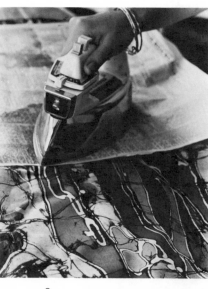

Technical Notes

The Cloth

A medium weight pure cotton or viscose rayon is probably the best kind of cloth to work with when first learning the technique, but batik can be done successfully on sheer fabrics (organdy, lawn), textured fabrics (corduroy, velvet), as well as linen and silk. If cloth is purchased at department store remnant counters, care must be taken to avoid any fabric with crease or soil-resistant finishes. These are chemical treatments which prevent the dyes from properly adhering to the fibers. White or any light color cloth can be used, with the realization that the background color will affect subsequent dyeing.

The choice of the cloth will depend, to some degree on the overall character and design of the work. For example, linen is appropriate for strong, bold images which are consistent with the fiber and weave of the fabric. A sharp, clearly defined crackle cannot be obtained on linen; if this final veining effect is wanted, cotton or silk should be used. For wall hangings, smoothly woven, medium weight fabrics are most suitable and can be of any appropriate fiber. Of the textured fabrics, cotton velvet is especially effective when combined with batik.

If an intensive amount of work is planned, it is suggested that the cloth be purchased directly from a supplier that specializes in untreated materials (Testfabrics, Inc. See page 114 for addresses.), thus assuring a consistency in the wax and dye applications. This fabric will not have any chemical finish and need only be washed.

Prior to dyeing, the cloth should always be washed in a hot soapy solution rather than a laundry detergent. Some craftsmen prefer washing the fabric for several minutes in boiling water to which washing soda (sal soda) has been added, approximately one-half ounce to one quart of water. This softens the fiber and removes any oil or sizing.

The cloth can be lightly ironed, if necessary. Starching is optional, although it is often recommended if an unusually clear crackle is wanted in the batik.

Dye manufacturers will sometimes also supply special detergents developed specifically as a pre-treatment for the cloth when using certain dyes. For best results, the fabric should be washed with these products.

Stretching the Fabric

Prior to waxing, the cloth should be stretched as tautly as possible so that the brush or tjanting tool can move freely over the surface. Curtain stretchers, notched adjustable frames and canvas stretcher frames are all suitable. Frames on stands, designed for rug-hooking, are also excellent for this purpose. A frame can easily be made from 1 x 2 pine, joined at the corners and sanded. Small areas of cloth can be waxed using an embroidery hoop for support.

When attaching the fabric to the frame, be certain to stretch only along the grain of the cloth, following a selvage or straight cut edge. Tack the cloth to the frame first at the corners, pulling evenly so that no buckling occurs. Large panels of fabric can be waxed in sections, changing the position of the cloth on the frame whenever necessary.

Some craftsmen prefer to place the fabric on a smooth table surface, with glass, wax paper or aluminum foil under the cloth. When the waxing is completed the cloth is carefully pulled away, although some wax is bound to adhere to the base material.

The stretcher frame has the advantage of allowing the wax to completely penetrate the cloth without leaving a residue on the work surface. If dyes are to be brushed on later, the frame is necessary to keep excess color from mingling underneath the work and to permit drying.

If stamping devices are used to apply the wax, the rigid support of a table surface will sometimes give better control as the tool is pressed into the cloth. This is especially true on medium to heavy weight fabrics. Many craftsmen, however, prefer to use stamping tools on a stretched fabric.

The Wax

The hot resist used in batik is usually a combination of two types of waxes melted together: paraffin, which is hard and brittle, and beeswax, which is soft and pliable. The formula is not exact but can vary anywhere from a fifty-fifty proportion to a ratio of three parts paraffin to one part beeswax. If paraffin alone is used, it is quite likely that the wax will chip off the cloth since it has very poor adhesion and thus readily cracks. The addition of beeswax counters this. Experience with different types of fabric is the best guide in determining the proper formula. It should be remembered that the greater the proportion of paraffin, the easier it will be to obtain a crackle effect in the last dye bath.

Paraffin is readily available in grocery stores where it can be purchased in one pound containers. Beeswax can be somewhat difficult to obtain locally; it can be quite expensive, as well. There is a commercially produced cake wax which is very similar to beeswax and can be substituted successfully for beeswax in any formula. In addition, it is relatively inexpensive. This is product #2305, available from the Mobil Oil Co. and other manufacturers of lubricants. Paraffin wax can also be purchased in large quantities directly from the manufacturer at great saving.

Details from batik wall hanging, *Red Floral* by Marion Bode. A richly textured surface results from crackle effects on cotton velveteen. Procion dyes in brilliant reds and black were used.

Mexican Eagle, a batik wall hanging on cotton with motifs adapted from Aztec symbolism. Direct dyes were used in orange, gold and red, with a final dye bath of black. (Marianne Vallet-Sandre)

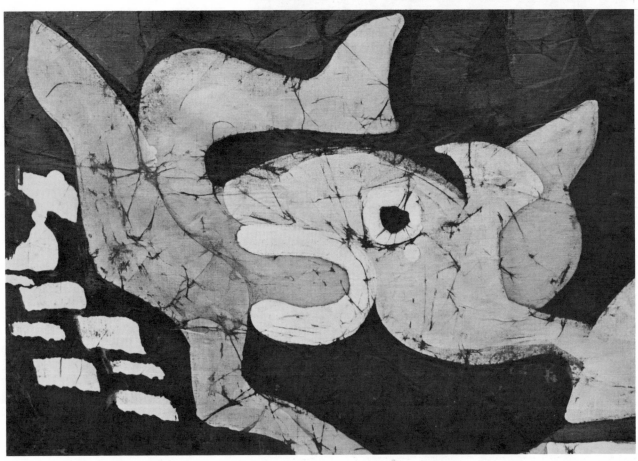

Heating the Wax

The wax formula is heated to a temperature of about 240°. With some stirring, the different waxes will mix together quite readily. The safest and most practical means of heating the wax is an electric fry pan. The thermostat setting keeps the wax always at the correct temperature, thus eliminating any concern about overheating or undue cooling.

Other methods of heating the wax can also be used. If working with a hotplate, put the pieces of wax into a light tin can, such as a one pound coffee can, and place this into a pan containing two or three inches of water on a low boil. A container with wax should never be placed directly on a burner element, since wax overheats quickly and will smoke. Some craftsmen keep the wax melted by inserting a 40 watt electric bulb directly into the container of wax.

Intelligent safety precautions should always be maintained when working with hot wax.

1. Set up the work area in a convenient manner so that the container heating the wax is close to the cloth and within easy arm reach.

2. Heat the wax in a container with an electric temperature control unit.

3. If a double boiler arrangement is used, heat the wax in the upper container and the water in the bottom section. Use a stove or hot plate with an electric heating element, never an exposed flame.

4. Do not use dyes or other liquids near hot wax. Any water dropped into hot wax will splatter.

5. Give attention to the wax while it is being heated.

6. When working with students or inexperienced adult groups, carefully explain the need for elementary precautions.

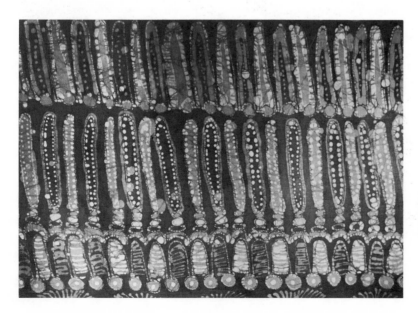

Rows of simple forms, each repeated in a slightly irregular manner form an appealing pattern surface. (Neil Tetkowski)

In this batik wall hanging on cotton, brushes were used to apply the wax in a free spontaneous manner. The quality of the brush stroke is always evident, giving character and definition to the forms. Direct dyes were used in both brush and dye bath methods on this large (72" x 36") panel. (Sarah Tobin)

Applying the Wax to the Cloth

Brushes. Several flat brushes of natural bristles, ranging in size from one half to three inches wide are necessary for applying the wax to the cloth. The one inch wide brush is especially practical if it has a diagonal cut to the bristles. Sometimes it is possible to purchase this type of brush. If not available, however, one may be made very easily by cutting diagonally across a standard brush with a sharp pair of shears. A fine delicate line can be made with this brush by using the point; wider lines can be made by using the side. The other brushes are used for shapes and textures of different kinds and filling-in of large areas.

The brush is placed in the pan of hot wax. Before it is taken to the cloth, the excess wax is pressed out by running the brush along the side of the pan. This prevents dripping. The brushes need not be cleaned after each use but they should be taken out of the pan of wax before it cools. Although the brush becomes hardened with wax its effectiveness is not impaired if the bristles are not distorted. At the next work session, when the wax is again melted, the brushes should be placed in the pan. After several minutes in the container of hot wax, they will soften and be ready to use.

The brushes can be cleaned by soaking in mineral spirits or commercial cleaning fluid to dissolve the wax.

Using the Tjanting Tool. The tjanting tool is very closely identified with the Javanese batik. To many craftsmen today, it is considered an optional tool, used primarily for special effects. Its proper use will produce a smoothly drawn line of wax, or characteristic dots and swirls.

As a little time is required to become familiar with the tool, it is advisable for the beginner to first practice on a spare piece of cloth. The open vessel in the tjanting which holds the wax should be filled to about three quarters, never completely full. This is best done with a spoon although some craftsmen prefer to dip the tool into the pan of melted wax. The wax should not be so hot that it runs out very rapidly and spreads when touching the cloth surface. It should flow out of the spout steadily, with little spreading beyond the drawn line.

The time factor is important in learning to use the tool with confidence. Any hesitance or indecision in applying the filled tjanting tool to the cloth will cause the wax to cool so that the line formed on the fabric turns whitish and rests on the surface of the cloth. The wax must penetrate the cloth if it is to provide a satisfactory resist to the dye.

While carrying the tjanting from the pan of wax to the batik cloth, drips will occur in even the most experienced hands. To prevent unwanted dots of wax forming on the fabric, hold a jar cap under the spout of the tool while it is being moved. A rag or paper towel can be substituted for this purpose.

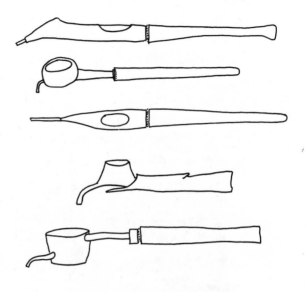

Various types of tjanting tools.

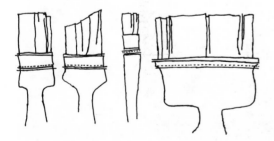

Different types of brushes used for applying wax.

Using Stamping Devices. For more regulated pattern effects, it is possible to make stamping devices which, like the Indonesian "tjap" tool, can press the wax motif into the cloth. Blocks of this type can easily be adapted from objects collected from many sources. For ease in handling, they should be mounted in a small block of wood or fitted with an improvised holder or handle.

Many simple objects can be used directly without any preliminary mounting. Ends of cardboard rolls, wooden thread spools, tin cans with the lids removed, are readily available and can be used for initial experiments with circular shapes. Kitchen tools and gadgets can also be used as stamps.

More specialized stamps can be made by cutting shapes from one quarter inch masonite board and attaching a section of dowel rod or a small piece of wood to serve as a handle. Since the masonite surface is not satisfactory for this type of printing (it absorbs the wax too quickly), a piece of heavy felt of the same shape should be glued to the bottom side. The felt is an ideal printing surface since it holds the hot wax long enough for a careful imprint to be made. Any type of shape which can be cut from the masonite on a band saw is suitable for this procedure.

When planning to make a stamp, select a base material that will hold the hot wax long enough for a satisfactory imprint to be made. Soft wood, masonite, and pressed board are too absorbent for direct printing; the wax cools too rapidly. For clear prints the surface of these materials must be covered with heavy felt. Metals, however, are excellent, since they retain the heat. Pre-cut shapes of copper or brass, can be used, as well as washers and bolts in many different sizes. For a holder attach a 3″ or 4″ length of dowel rod with epoxy glue.

A group of stamping tools cut from masonite, with felt attached to the surface of the shape. The handles are of wood.

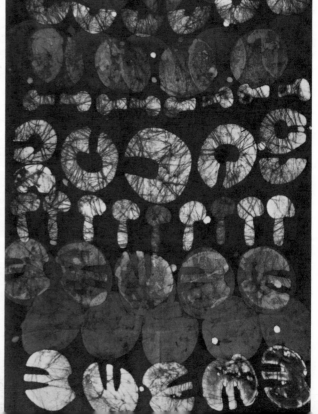

Samples showing different ways the stamping tools might be used.
(Peter Sloan)

Simple blocks can be made by hammering rows of large nails onto a wood base. The base should be of a size that can be held easily in the hand, thus functioning as a holder. The nail heads form the pattern. The block is held with the nail heads submerged in the hot wax for several seconds. Allow the excess wax to drip back into the container before carrying the stamp to the cloth for printing. Other small objects can be mounted in a similar way. It is necessary to first experiment on small sections of fabric to discover the most effective use of any stamping device.

A small Indian wood block was used as a stamp to apply the wax. (Cynthia Bainbridge)

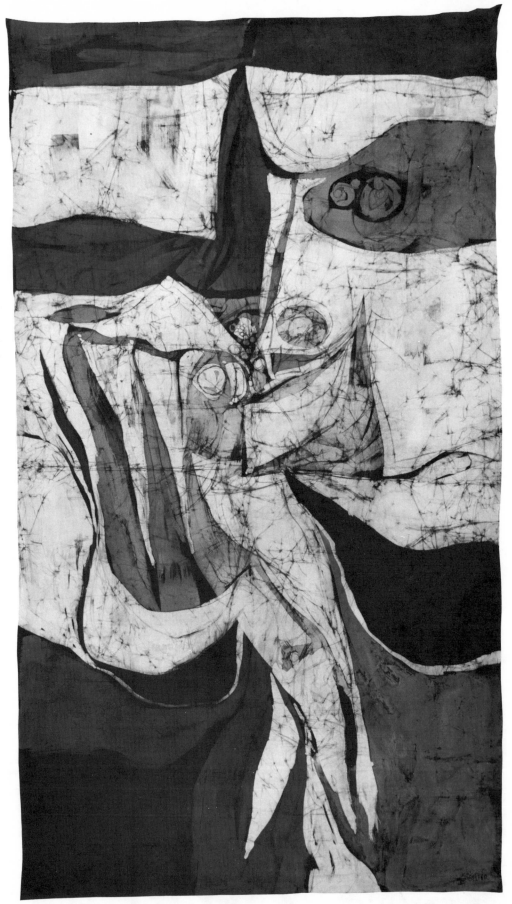

Earth Forms. Batik on cotton, 62'' x 36''. In this wall hanging, direct dyes in yellows, orange and blue were applied with brushes after the initial blocking in of the wax shapes. Prior to the final dye bath of brown, the cloth was crushed to obtain the allover crackle surface.

Crackle and Special Effects

The network of linear markings scattered over the surface of a batik cloth has become so characteristic of the process, it is almost its first means of identification. These web-like lines occur wherever the smooth surface of the wax is broken, thus allowing the dye to enter the cloth. Deliberate crushing or folding of the cloth prior to immersion in the dye bath will result in crackle formations.

Crackle effects, although used a great deal, should not be thought of as uniform or automatic since their placement and density can be controlled without too much difficulty. It may be that no crackle at all is wanted; in that case the greater proportion of the wax formula should be beeswax or its commercial soft wax equivalent.

The beginner should be cautioned against too much crackle, as this can overpower the color and shape effects previously established within the design. With some experience it will be possible to control the use of crackle so that it truly enhances the total effectiveness of the work. Regardless of whether the dipping or brushing procedure is used in building the design, the crackle is usually obtained in the last dye bath—in most cases, a dark color.

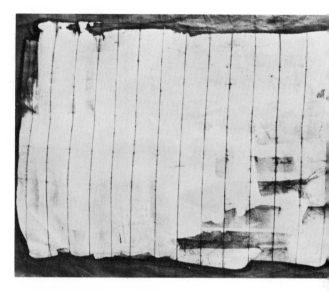

For a fine crackle, it is suggested that the cloth be chilled, so that the wax will be as hard as possible. If convenient, empty a tray of ice cubes into a filled sink or large pan of water. Place the waxed cloth, folded, in this bath for about five minutes. Cold tap water will suffice if ice is not available. Remove the cloth from the bath and unfold it. To break the surface of the wax, crush it several times from different angles. Do not be overly energetic in doing this or sections of wax may chip off. For a very light crackle, the normal compressing of the cloth to fit the dye bath will probably be sufficient.

Carefully pull the crumpled cloth back into its original shape and fold gently for immersion in the dye bath. Be certain to leave the cloth in the dye bath long enough—at least thirty minutes, although some craftsmen advise an overnight dye bath for a strong crackle. Rinse the cloth and dry thoroughly (at least one hour) before ironing out the wax.

Sample showing fold lines made in the wax before the dye bath.

Linear Effects: Folding. If a fairly controlled linear effect is wanted in the batik, it is possible to fold the cloth so that a series of lines, rather than a random crackle, is formed as the wax cracks. These lines are then dyed into the cloth.

The directions for chilling the cloth are the same, but instead of crushing, the fabric is precisely folded so that the wax is cracked in a straight line. Work slowly, gently firming the fold line as it is made. These folds can be parallel, radial or variable and of differing directions and lengths. This technique is probably most effective when confined to certain sections of the piece, rather than utilized as an all-over surface effect.

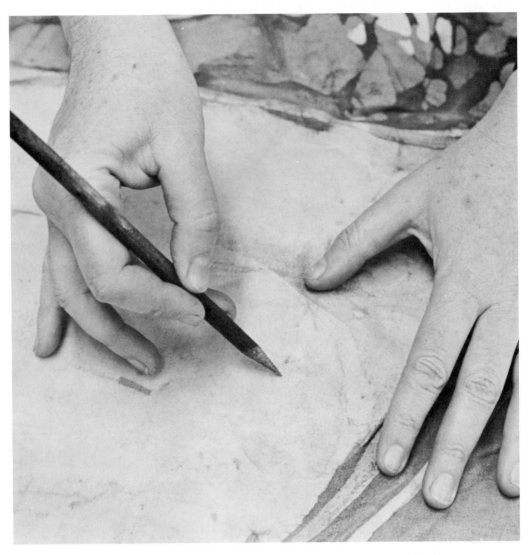

Drawing lines into the wax with a sharpened section of dowel rod.

Linear Effects: Drawing into the Wax. Before the last dye bath, it is possible to actually draw or scratch linear markings into the wax, which are then permanently dyed into the cloth. Here again, this is a technique best utilized in one or two areas of the work.

The tool for this drawing or sgraffito can be improvised, as long as the marking point is smooth and there is no danger of accidentally tearing the cloth. A section of ¼" dowel rod, sharpened to a point and lightly sanded, works very well, as do some brush handle tips.

Detail of completed batik showing the linear effects obtained by drawing into the wax surface.

Removing the Wax

The removal of the wax is usually done in two stages, ironing and dry cleaning.

The ironing of a large batik is most efficiently done on the floor or on a worktable surface where layers of newspapers can be built up to a thickness of about one-fourth inch. The newspapers should be at least a week old so the ink is thoroughly dry and will not stain the cloth. Newsprint pads and paper towels can also be used for this purpose. Place the batik on the bed of papers, placing one sheet of paper over the top surface. With the iron set according to the correct cloth temperature, move it slowly over the top layer of paper. The melting wax will be absorbed by the paper. When the top sheet of paper is stained with wax, lift it off and discard it, discarding as well the paper directly beneath the fabric. Repeat this procedure until the papers no longer absorb the wax.

The cloth will be stiff at this point, since the ironing does not remove all of the wax. In addition, rings of wax will show on the cloth where a dyed section is next to a waxed shape in the design. To remove all of the wax, soak the cloth for a short time in a solvent which will dissolve whatever wax still remains in the fabric. The safest solvents to use for this purpose are those prepared for dry cleaning, purchased from department stores or from suppliers to commercial dry cleaners.

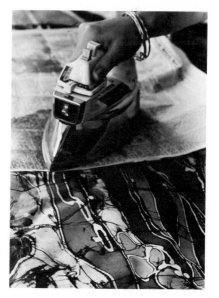

Paint thinners, such as benzine or mineral spirits, can also be used to dissolve the wax but these are highly inflammable and must be used with extreme caution, never near an open flame or cigarette.

After using a solvent, do not iron the batik until it has thoroughly dried and the fumes have evaporated.

Unless the dyes used are known to be permanent, it is not recommended that wax be removed by boiling off since doing so could result in drastic color loss.

47

The Dyes

There are several kinds of dyes available which are appropriate for use in batik work. They are, for the most part, fairly simple to use and do not call for the addition of toxic chemicals. The craftsman should be familiar with these different types of dyes in order to select the one which has an affinity for the particular cloth fiber being used. Dyes vary in chemical composition and because of this, each dye reacts differently with variations in fiber content.

There is little analogy between the commercial use of dyes by the textile industry and the use of dyes by the craftsman in his own studio. When millions of yards of fabric are involved, every aspect of the dyeing procedure is completely scientific, with numerous factors considered in planning. Temperatures and rate of heating are controlled exactly; carefully measured chemical agents are periodically added to facilitate the dyeing.

When dyes are used in batik work and related dye processes, it should be remembered that some basic guides can be given for mixing and preparing the colors; however, there are too many variables involved for exact formulas to be valid. Dyes prepared as brushing solutions will naturally be more concentrated than dye bath mixtures. The proportions given here will be suitable for brushing. Tests should be made on small pieces of cloth of the same fiber content as that used in the batik, to be certain the color obtained is satisfactory.

Normal dyeing procedures usually call for a prolonged hot bath, a simmer, until the colorative material in the dye bath is exhausted or absorbed into the fiber of the cloth. In batik work, this procedure will not be possible, since the heat of the dye bath would melt the wax and thus destroy the image. The temperature of the dye bath should be approximately 100°-110°F. While some wax formulas can withstand a higher temperature it is best to be within a safe range. Certain dyes which are ordinarily used in hot baths can be allowed to cool and can be used for batik work if the strength of the dye is increased as compensation.

The various types of dyes described here will serve as a guide to selection and usage. Since all dye colors of a particular type can intermix, it is not necessary to purchase all of the colors listed by the manufacturer. A wide range of colors can be mixed from the following:

Reds—scarlet red (red toward orange)
magenta red (red toward violet)

Yellows—lemon yellow (yellow toward green)
deep yellow (yellow toward orange)

Blues—ultramarine blue (blue toward violet)
turquoise blue (blue toward green)

Brown and **Black** are optional

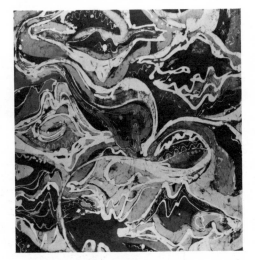

On a square of cotton muslin, 40" x 40", a beginning student, with no pre-planning, freely explores the various ways of applying wax and dyes.
(Nancy Wilford)

The poignant nostalgia of three aging ladies in a chorus line is expressed by Diane King in this batik wall hanging, *Three Dancers.* Procion dyes were used on cotton.

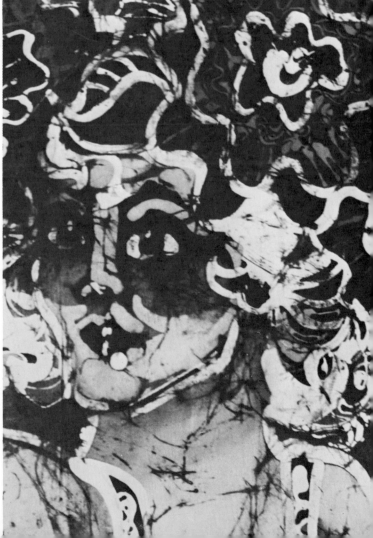

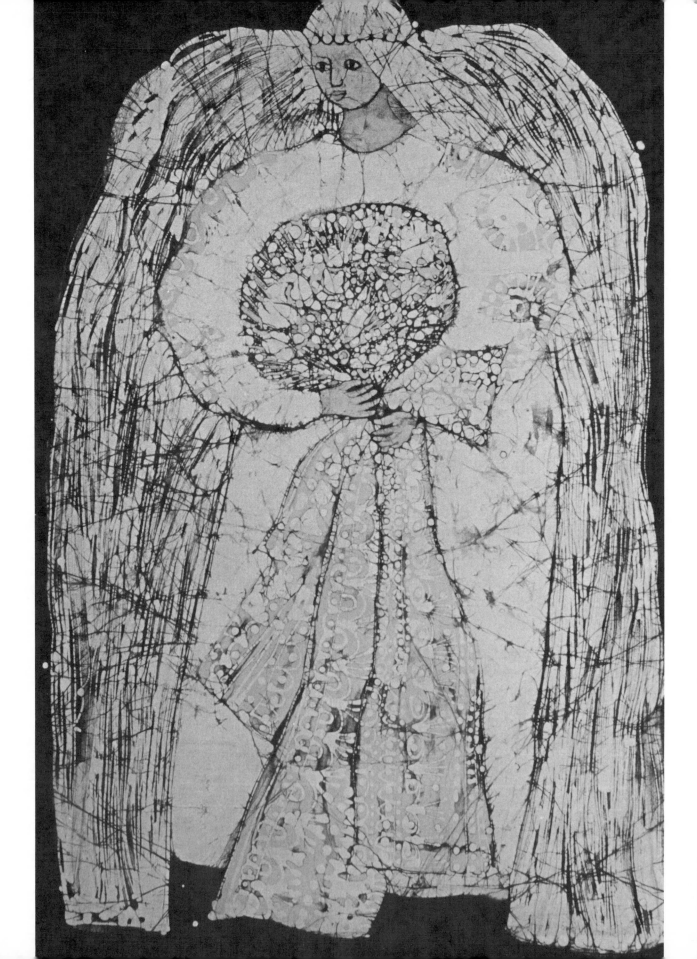

These colors are described in a very general way because most manufacturers develop their own terminology to identify their particular line of colors. Sometimes a number or letter coding system is used. These names and codes are often confusing if a color chart is not available. When ordering dyes from this type of listing, write to the supplier if there are any doubts as to the exact nature of the color.

Dyes are usually prepared and are purchased in powder form. Prior to mixing the dye bath, it is necessary to first "paste" or thoroughly mash the measured amount of the dye in a small amount of cool water. Using a flat stick, a small spatula or a spoon, stir the mixture carefully so that all of the color particles are dissolved. Then, add hot or boiling water and stir. The dye bath solution should be clear, not cloudy.

In preparing dye baths, soft water is preferable, so "Calgon" is added in the proportion of one teaspoon to each quart of liquid. Some dyes will require additional additives, such as common salt or acetic acid. It should be noted that only dyes which do not require potentially harmful chemicals are listed here. Dyes requiring the addition of sulphuric acid or caustic soda (lye) to the formula are not included. However, many kinds of dyes with fine color quality are available and can be used with relative ease and safety.

For all dye baths use pans of stainless steel or enamel ware; galvanized metal will corrode. Brushing solutions are best kept in glass jars with covers; covered plastic or glass containers are used for storage of dye mixtures.

The types of dyes described here can be used for batik, as well as other resist-dye processes. Remember to allow the dye bath to cool sufficiently (100°F.) before immersing the waxed batik cloth. More specialized information pertaining specifically to the use of dyes in tie-dye methods will be found on page 88.

Although some sources and manufacturers are briefly indicated here, complete addresses will be found in the listing of suppliers on page 114.

Household Dyes or All-Purpose Dyes. Household or all-purpose dyes are probably the most familiar of all dye substances. They are mixtures of different types of dyes, which are effective on several kinds of fibers. Thus, the same dye will have an affinity for cotton, linen, viscose rayon, wool and silk.

The dyes are easy to use and some brands (Rit, Tintex) are available in department stores packaged in small envelopes. Of this type of dye, Cushing Dyes can be highly recommended for excellence in color quality and ease in use. They are available by mail order in packets, half pound and pound containers. The packet is the most expensive way to purchase dye; the pound container, the most economical.

Many colors are available and care is necessary in making selections so that hues of the best intensity are obtained. Intermediate tones can easily be mixed. A color chart is available.

In the wall hanging, *Bride,* Morag Benepe utilizes to best advantage the unique textural qualities of the wax to portray the poetic white-veiled figure.

The directions on the package apply to yardage dyeing and should not be followed when preparing dyes for batik and tie dye resist dyeing. A general formula can be used which can be adjusted according to individual requirements. A strong solution, suitable for direct brushing, is prepared as follows:

Paste: 1 teaspoon dye in a small amount of cool water

Add: 1-2 pints boiling water

or

add hot water and bring the solution to boiling

Test the color on small pieces of fabric, of the same fiber content that will be used later. Keep the test pieces for records. Adjust the solution according to the strength of color wanted, either by increasing the amount of dye or by adding additional water.

This solution can be extended to a one quart dye bath timed at thirty-forty-five minutes. If the fabric requires more than one quart of water for adequate coverage, additional dye should be added proportionally. For dark colors, add one-half cup salt after the first fifteen minutes. The cloth is removed, the salt stirred in, and the cloth returned to the dye bath for the appropriate length of time.

For light and medium tones, the excess dye can be rinsed away after the dye bath. Use cool water. The colors will be deeper (more intense) if the cloth is first dried, then carefully rinsed in cool water and dried again.

Direct Dyes. Direct dyes are especially formulated for use on cellulosic fibers: cotton, linen, and viscose rayon, although they can also be used on silk and wool. The color range is excellent and intermixing can extend even further the number of hues obtained. The colors are reasonably fast to light but should not be subjected to boiling. Direct dyes require the addition of salt as the exhaust agent.

Some dye manufacturers (Ciba-Geigy, Du Pont, etc.) prepare dyes for industrial purposes only; these products cannot be purchased by individuals

On a yellow cloth background, bold flower and leaf forms in oranges and greens (household dyes) make a striking wall panel. (Deanna Donatelli)

in small quantities. Keystone Aniline Co., however, has a range of direct dyes which can be purchased by the pound. Several companies have prepared lines of direct dyes, with directions especially formulated for use in batik work. These dyes are available by the pound or in smaller quantities from Fezandie & Sperrle, Craftool, Inc., and Bachmeier, Inc.

The method of preparing a concentrated dye solution suitable for brushing is as follows:

Paste: 1 teaspoon dye in a small amount of cool water

Add: 1 to 2 pints hot water

      3 tablespoons salt

Heat the solution to boiling, stir thoroughly, and allow to cool.

The procedure for testing the color, extending and adjusting the formula for dye baths, and for rinsing, is essentially the same as that recommended for the all-purpose dyes.

Acid Dyes. Acid dyes are especially prepared for use on silk and wool and have an immediate affinity for these fibers. They are available in a complete color range; additional colors can be obtained by intermixing. While acid dyes are reasonably fast to light, they should not be subjected to boiling. The dyes are available from Keystone Aniline Co., Fezandie & Sperrle, Craftool, Inc., and Bachmeier.

A brushing solution is prepared as follows:

Paste: 1 teaspoon dye powder in a small amount of warm water

Add: 1-2 pints hot water

      2 tablespoons salt

      1 tablespoon acetic acid (if vinegar is used as a substitute,
        double the amount)

Heat, and stir thoroughly, but do not boil.

The procedure for testing the color, extending and adjusting the formula for dye baths, and for rinsing, is essentially the same as that recommended for the dyes listed above.

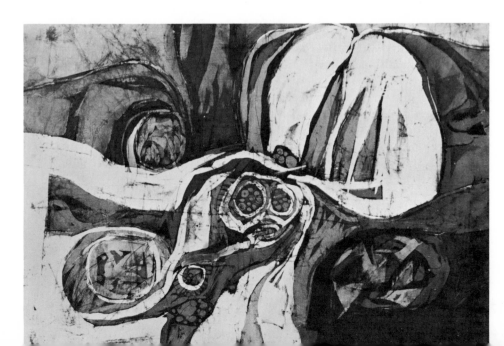

A batik wall panel, 28" x 44", in blue, violet, orange and brown tones.

Basic Dyes. Basic dyes produce very brilliant colors but, unfortunately, will fade rapidly when exposed to sunlight. These dyes are effective when used in small areas as accents, but can be used in larger amounts if the cloth is used in areas with artificial rather than natural illumination.

Basic dyes have an affinity for silk and wool and can be used directly on these fibers. For use on cotton, linen, and viscose rayon, a mordant is necessary, prior to dyeing. This can be done in two ways:

1. Dye the cloth with direct dyes, using the standard method of simmering (180°-200°F.) for about 45 minutes. This will serve to mordant the cloth, giving an affinity for the basic dyes.

2. Soak the cloth in a mordant bath. For one quart liquid, dissolve 2 ounces tannic acid in a small amount of hot water, add to cool bath and stir. Enter the cloth and heat to 120°-140°F. for about 2 hours. Allow to cool; the fabric remains in the solution overnight. Then, without rinsing, place the cloth in another bath containing 1 ounce tartar emetic and 1 quart water. Soak for 15-30 minutes, rinse and dry.

For a brushing mixture:

Paste: 1 teaspoon dye powder in a small amount of acetic acid

Add: 1-2 pints hot water

Heat the mixture, but do not boil; stir thoroughly.

Testing is very important when using basic dyes. They are extremely brilliant, so intense that they can easily overpower other types of dye colors used in the piece. They are probably most effective when used alone, rather than in combination with other dye colors, or, when a small amount is applied as a special accent.

Basic dyes cannot be intermixed with direct or acid dyes in liquid solutions.

Reactive or Procion^{TM} Dyes. Reactive or Procion (trademark of I.C.I. Organics, Ltd.) dyes offer a range of very brilliant colors which can be used in cool baths for batik. When prepared with the correct additives, the dyes are permanently bonded to the fiber and are thus fast to light and washing. The colors will intermix without graying and have affinity for cotton, viscose rayon, linen and silk. They are available by the pound and in smaller quantities from several companies noted in the listing of suppliers.

As in the preparation of all dye mixtures, the proportions will vary according to the strength of color that is wanted. Directions for yardage dyeing with Procion dyes usually require well over an hour, but by increasing the amount of dye, the time can be shortened to 20-30 minutes. Colors should be tested on small pieces of cloth to observe the strength of the color when dry.

A strong dye solution suitable for brushing is prepared as follows:

Paste: 1-2 teaspoons dye in a small amount of cool water

Add: 1-2 pints hot tap water

6 tablespoons salt

Stir, allowing the salt to dissolve

Add: 2 tablespoons of washing soda, dissolved in a small amount of warm water.

This brushing mixture can be extended to a 1 quart dye bath. Place the cloth in the bath, turning it frequently, for about five minutes before adding the washing soda. After the soda is added, continue the dyeing for about fifteen-twenty minutes. For lengths of fabric requiring more than 1 quart of water for a dye bath, increase the amount of the dye to other additives proportionally.

The addition of the washing soda activates the dye for about six hours. If used after this time, the color will be lightfast but will not withstand washing.

Decorative fabric patterned in soft gold tones with orange. Acid dyes on silk. (Carol Edwards)

Detail of large wall hanging using direct and basic dyes on cotton.

(Left) Detail of sarong. (Below) Border details. All designs are batik on cotton from Java. 20th century.

Earth Form II.
Batik on cotton,
65'' X 42''.

Plant Study.
Batik on viscose
rayon, 36″ X 40″.

Batik designs on
cotton. (Right)
Detail of design by
Lucille Licata.
(Far right) Detail of
Ferns by Sarah Tobin.

Growth. Batik on cotton, 24″ X 36″.

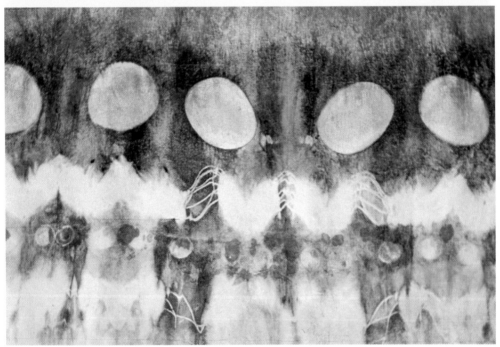

Details of tie dye on viscose rayon.

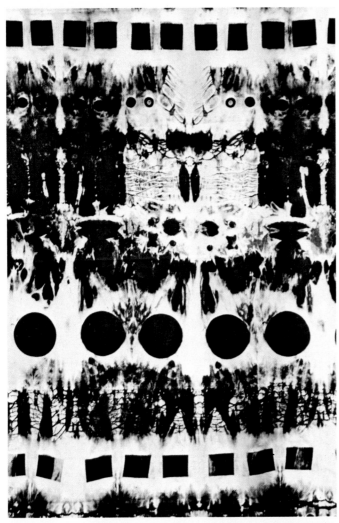

(Left) Detail, discharge dyeing on cotton. (Below) Detail, tie die on viscose satin.

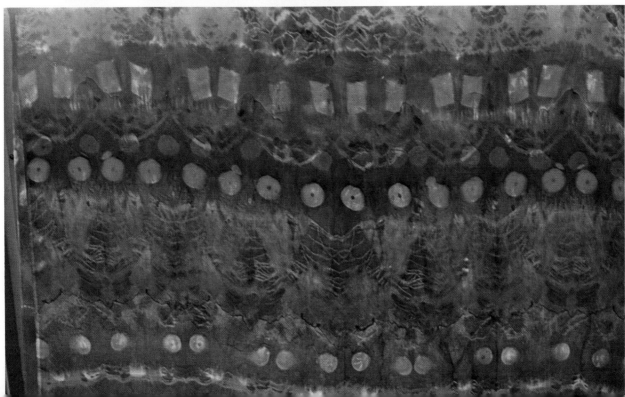

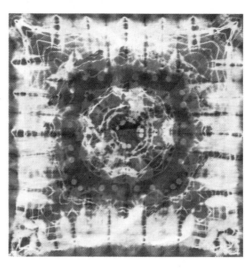

(Above and left)
Samples of tie dye
designs on cotton.

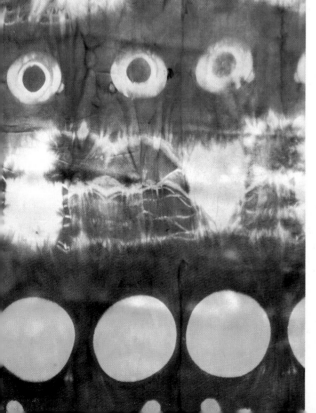

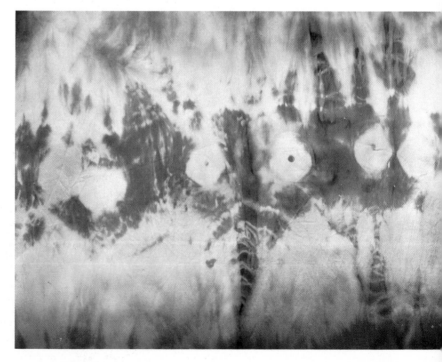

(Above and left)
Details of tie dye
designs on viscose satin.

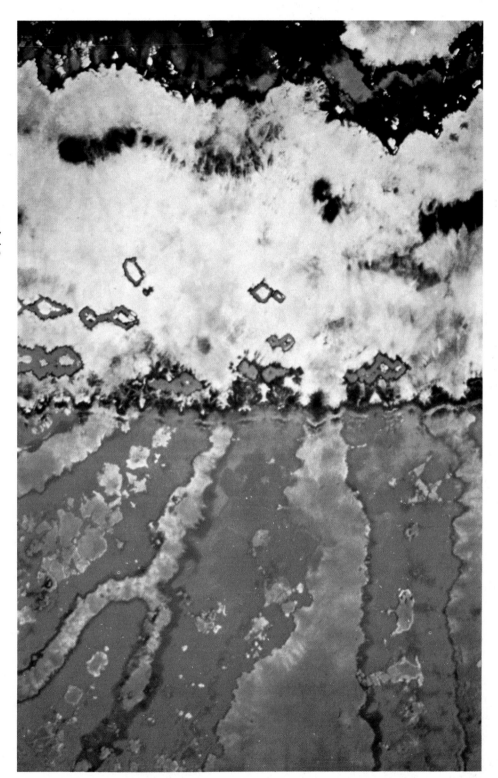

Red Horizon.
Tie dye on silk,
68″ X 42″.
(Marion Clayden)

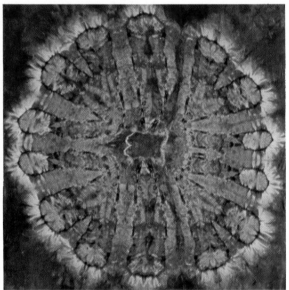

Tie dye designs on silk.
(Carter Smith)

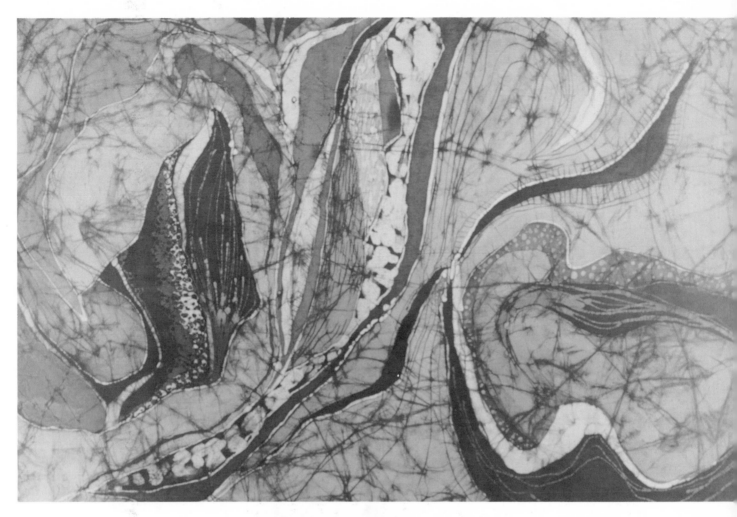

Organic shapes adapted from the
forms of sea shells offer many
opportunities for variation in
applying the wax. (Maribeth Frey)

In using Procion dyes, it is important to note that the cloth should not be rinsed until 24 hours have elapsed after the final dye bath. This is a necessary part of the fixing process when a short, concentrated dye bath is used, as it would be in batik and other resist-dye techniques.

With these dyes, the wax does not hold firmly in the cloth for more than two dye baths. A solution is to combine both direct brush and dipping methods in the same piece. The wax can be removed by ironing in the usual way. Excess wax can be removed with a solvent or by boiling off.

Vat Dyes. Vat dyes are very permanent, fast to light and washing. For liquid baths, however, they require the preparation of a chemical vatting solution prior to dyeing. Some of these dyes are not soluble in water and call for the use of chemicals potentially dangerous to the inexperienced craftsman. *Fabric Printing by Hand* by Stephen Russ gives specific directions for their use.

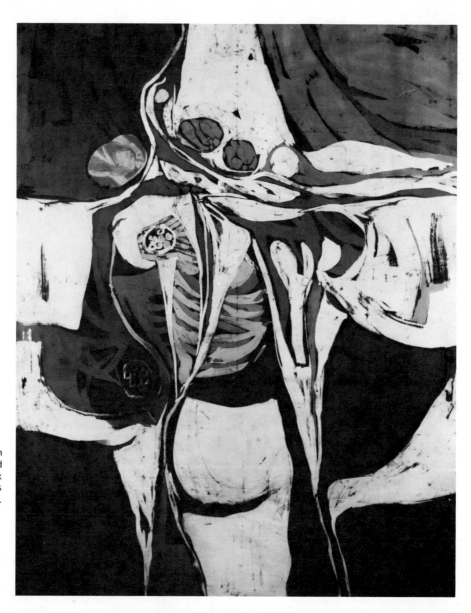

Indian Summer, 54" x 42". An arrangement of bold shapes and vibrant colors in a cotton batik wall hanging. Procion dyes were used.

Bird of Fantasy, 24" x 40". A stylized bird form in yellows and greens, with some red.

Far easier to use, however, are the prepared vat dyes available in clear paste form in a wide range of colors. These are known as "Inkodyes" and are obtained from Screen Process Supplies Mfg. Co. In batik work, they can be used as brushing solutions applied directly to the cloth; after drying, additional waxing can be done, and a different color brushed on. If crackling is wanted, the cloth is crushed, pulled apart, and the dye applied either by brushing or with a sponge.

The colors can be used directly from the container or thinned by mixing with a clear base which will result in a lighter and more transparent value.

The advantage of these dyes is their permanence. When fixed, they will withstand boiling. Also, they can be brushed directly onto the cloth before any waxing is done, with a minimum of spreading. When dried and developed, the areas can be waxed over, with additional dyeing and waxing occurring later. This allows for great spontaneity in the development of the design.

The disadvantage of this type of dye is that the actual color is not apparent while the work is being done. When the dyes are applied, they are in clear paste form; the colors develop gradually by exposure to strong sunlight (this will not disturb the wax) or by ironing while still damp (this will melt out the wax as well as develop the dye). Colors should be pretested on small pieces of cloth to observe how they will develop.

These dyes offer an interesting departure from liquid dyes, although it is not possible to actually "see" the color while working. Detailed instructions are available from the manufacturer.

59

Applying the Dyes

Dye Baths. The traditional manner of applying the dye to the cloth is by immersing the entire fabric in the prepared bath of color. For the initial dye bath, the cloth should be handled very carefully so that the wax application is not disturbed. Light folding is best. First place the cloth in cool water for several minutes until it is evenly wetted out; then lift it out, allowing the excess water to drip off. The fabric can then be placed in the prepared dye bath for the correct length of time necessary to achieve the desired color. This is determined by tests made on small pieces of the same cloth being used in the batik.

A pan large enough to accommodate the entire fabric is necessary. The cloth should be gently moved about while in the dye bath so that the color penetrates evenly, without unwanted streaking. Wear rubber gloves while turning or lifting the cloth. Since the fabric will always seem much darker when wet, time the bath accordingly.

Review the rinsing procedures for the particular dye being used; for example, Procion dyes should not be rinsed until twenty-four hours have elapsed. When lifting the cloth from the dye bath, hold it over the pan so the excess dye drips back. If the color is not exhausted, the dye can be used again as a lighter value or it can be used as the basis for mixing a new color. Do not wring the cloth as this might break the wax. The rinse bath should be tepid rather than cold water.

After rinsing, spread the cloth out to dry on newspapers or a sheet of plastic. It is also possible to hang the cloth to dry by fastening with clothespins on one end. Do not double the fabric over the clothesline as a streak will result at the line. If Procion dyes are used, always dry the cloth on a flat surface.

After the first color is completely dry, the cloth can be tacked once more to the stretcher frame. Examine the initial waxing carefully. It may be necessary to rewax or touch-up some areas where unwanted cracking has occurred. If there seems to be an unusual amount of cracking, add more soft wax or beeswax to the formula.

At this stage the batik is ready for the second waxing. If sketching is necessary use charcoal. Wax is now applied to all areas of the cloth that are to retain the first color. The brushes and tjanting tool can be used in the same manner as before. Check the back of the cloth to be certain the wax penetrates properly; it may be necessary to apply wax to the reverse side, as well.

When the waxing is complete, prepare the second dye bath in the usual manner. It should be remembered that the second color will be affected by the first, and it should be selected accordingly. For example, if yellow is the first color, and red the second, the color obtained will be orange. In over-dyeing, however, value as well as hue is important, so it is wise to make a preliminary test on a corner of the cloth to be certain the desired color is obtained.

The design for this batik wall panel was based
on an arrangement of orange and watermelon
slices. (Gloria Smith)

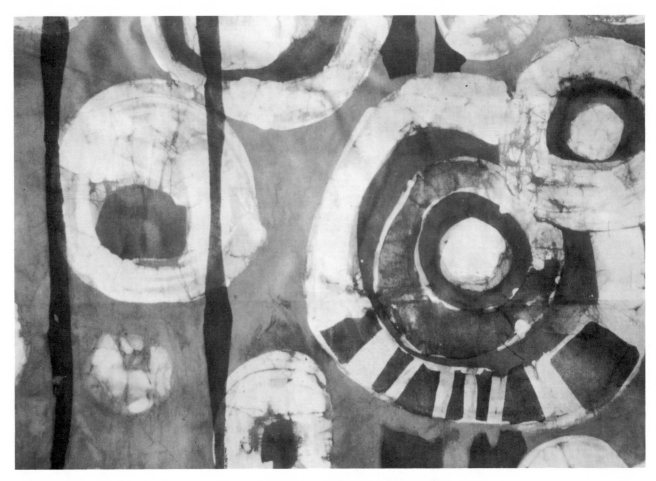

Strong forms, reminiscent of enormous flowers,
interrelate with lines in this detail of a
batik wall hanging on cotton.

This procedure of waxing and dyeing can be repeated several more times. The cloth is usually crushed prior to the last dye bath if a crackle effect is desired.

When working with dye baths, the following points should be noted:

1. Before entering the cloth, check the temperature of the dye bath with a thermometer.

2. If it is necessary to add additional dye to strengthen the dye bath, remove the fabric, add the pasted dye (never dry powder), stir thoroughly, and return the fabric.

3. For stronger color, allow the fabric to dry first, then rinse off excess dye and dry again.

4. Handle the cloth very carefully to prevent unwanted cracking and chipping of the wax.

If the batik is unusually large in size or on a very bulky fabric, such as velvet or wool, it may not be possible to find a pan large enough to accommodate it. If this is the case, the cloth can be dyed in sections. For convenience, this is best done on the floor or on a large table surface protected with newspapers. Fold the fabric lengthwise in half or in thirds and place one of the end sections in the dye bath, moving it about from time to time, until the proper color is obtained. The first section is lifted out of the bath and the next section put into the dye, with a slight overlapping. This continues until the entire fabric has been dyed.

It is important that all sections of the cloth be immersed in the dye bath for an equal amount of time; this insures uniform absorption of the color. This procedure can be quite time-consuming, but it is sometimes the only way a large or very bulky fabric can be properly dyed.

Allow the cloth to dry before rinsing out the excess dye.

Direct Brush Application of Dyes. The application of the dyes with brushes, directly on to the stretched cloth, is a departure from traditional methods. After the initial blocking-in of shapes and lines with the wax, the colors are applied within areas or "islands" enclosed by the wax.

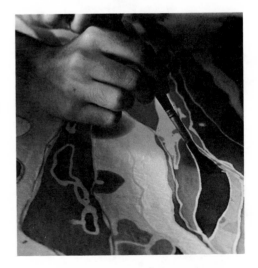

This is a technique which offers many possibilities in color usage, since several colors can be initially applied to the white cloth and when dry, retained with wax. Using the dyes in this manner allows for a more varied overall color imagery because the number of tonal variations possible through subsequent waxing and over-dyeing is so much greater.

For example, after the first wax application, dyes in blue, green and red are brushed directly onto unwaxed shapes in the cloth. Each color is retained within a wax boundary. Some of the shapes can be left undyed, thus remaining white. When the dyes have dried completely, further wax applications can indicate additional variations in shape, line and textural surface. At this stage, new colors can be brushed on, or the entire fabric can be placed in a dye bath. A simple solution might be a dye bath of

63

Objects combining ceramic and stuffed batik forms of velvet, designed by Doris Andrie.

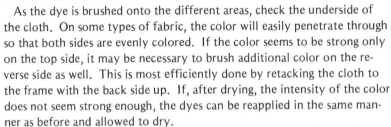

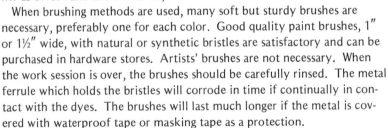

deep yellow: over the unwaxed red, orange would result; over the unwaxed blue, green would result; over the unwaxed green, yellow-green would result. Remaining areas of the cloth with neither wax nor dye will be dyed yellow. After drying, there could be additional waxing, controlled crackling, and a final dye bath in a dark color, perhaps purple or brown.

For brushing methods, the dyes should be strong concentrations which can be stored safely in covered jars. Direct, acid and all-purpose dyes can be warmed prior to use by inserting an electric coil heater into the jar for a few minutes. If the dye solution looks cloudy, boil it through again until it clears.

As the dye is brushed onto the different areas, check the underside of the cloth. On some types of fabric, the color will easily penetrate through so that both sides are evenly colored. If the color seems to be strong only on the top side, it may be necessary to brush additional color on the reverse side as well. This is most efficiently done by retacking the cloth to the frame with the back side up. If, after drying, the intensity of the color does not seem strong enough, the dyes can be reapplied in the same manner as before and allowed to dry.

When brushing methods are used, many soft but sturdy brushes are necessary, preferably one for each color. Good quality paint brushes, 1" or 1½" wide, with natural or synthetic bristles are satisfactory and can be purchased in hardware stores. Artists' brushes are not necessary. When the work session is over, the brushes should be carefully rinsed. The metal ferrule which holds the bristles will corrode in time if continually in contact with the dyes. The brushes will last much longer if the metal is covered with waterproof tape or masking tape as a protection.

Some craftsmen prefer to apply the dyes directly to the cloth with small sponges or pieces of absorbent cotton, rather than brushes. The method is the same as described for brush usage, with the dyes applied to shapes isolated by the wax. For the final color, where the crackle effect is obtained, the cloth is usually immersed in a dye bath.

64

In applying the dyes directly to the cloth, some craftsmen prefer to work with dye pastes, rather than liquid dyes. In paste form, dyes can be applied to the fabric, prior to waxing, without undue spreading of color. Vat dyes, in prepared pastes, have been described earlier. With Procion dyes, however, it is possible to purchase a paste activator (Pylam Products) which will form a paste when mixed with the proper amount of water. The dye powder is stirred into the paste. This can be applied to the cloth with brushes or small sponges. In addition, dye paste mixtures are available from suppliers for use with direct and acid dyes.

Batik doll form by Morag Benepe.

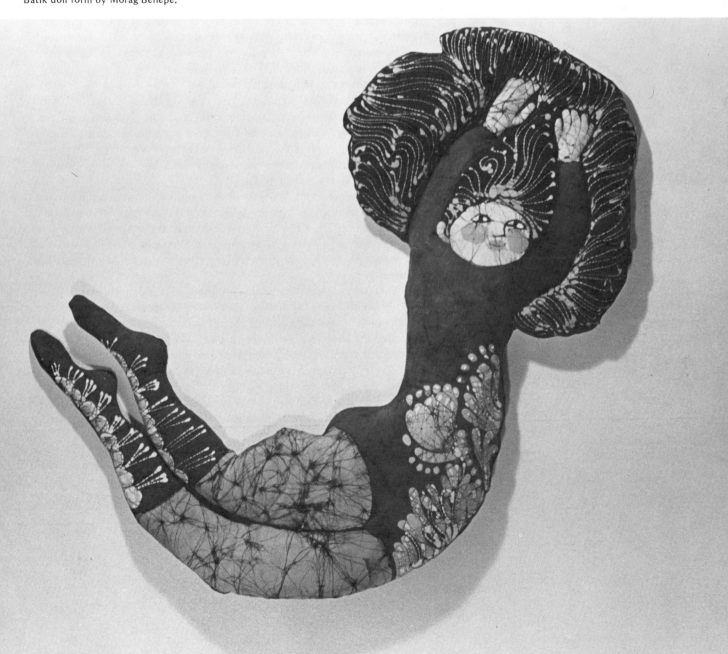

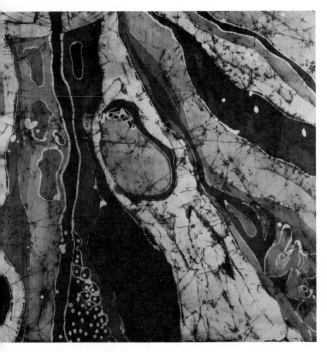

Detail of batik using brush
methods to apply the dye.
(Lucille Licata)

Setting the Color

When dyes are used in warm rather than hot baths, as they would be for batik, a curing procedure is usually necessary to set the color. The ironing of the fabric for wax removal helps somewhat in this regard but a steaming of about one hour is also recommended.

Any large deep pot can be adapted for use as a steamer for this type of color fixation. The wide enamel kettles used to sterilize bottles are ideal. They are available in most hardware stores and are easy to use since the metal rack can be turned upside down to form a supporting shelf for the cloth. If a rack is not available, a supporting grid can be improvised by setting four tin cans of the same height around the bottom of the pot, evenly spaced. A round, flat metal cake rack is then placed over the cans to form the shelf.

About fifteen to twenty layers of newspaper are placed over the shelf. Measure the diameter of the pot and cut the circles of newspaper about one inch less. A circle of heavy felt should also be cut to the same size. The newspaper and felt are placed on the shelf, centered, so that the sides of the pot are not touched. This will prevent splashing drops of boiling water from accidentally wetting the fabric.

The cloth should be lightly rolled in newspaper, then turned in to form a coil and lightly tied off. Unless printing pastes have been used there is no danger of unwanted color transferring from one layer of fabric to another, so it is possible to fold the cloth once or twice before rolling it in the paper. Keep the packet as loosely wrapped as possible to allow the steam to enter all layers of the fabric.

In a container of this type, about three to four inches of boiling water will provide steam for over one hour. Do not place the cloth bundle in the container until the water has boiled and the chamber has filled with steam. For a cover use a piece of thick carpet padding rather than the metal lid. The padding will absorb droplets of water and also allow the excess steam to escape.

When steam is in the container, remove the lid and quickly place the cloth bundle inside. If there is room several bundles can be steamed at the same time. Some additional pieces of felt or paper towelling can be put around the bundles. The lid should be returned to position as quickly as possible. The usual fixing time is for one hour but this time is often extended, especially when treating large or bulky pieces of fabric. If there is any doubt that the steam did not circulate freely enough to evenly penetrate all layers of the cloth, the piece can be rewrapped and the entire process repeated. After removing the fabric from the steam container, untie the cord and immediately remove the wrapping.

This procedure is generally appropriate for fabrics dyed with direct, acid, basic, or household dyes. Reactive or Procion dyes may also be treated in this manner but do not require as long a time span—thirty to forty-five minutes is adequate. More specialized fixing procedures are described in the section on different types of dyes; these would apply specifically to one particular type of dye.

Placing the wrapped batik cloth in the steamer.

Mordant Rinse. Another method of setting dye colors in batik and tie dye work is by soaking the cloth in a mordant solution. This is called a hydro-rinse or top-mordanting. It is done after the dyeing has been completed and is recommended by some dye manufacturers.

Soak the fabric for 30 to 45 minutes in a solution of:

2 ounces alum
1 ounce cream of tartar
2 gallons water

     or

2% tannic acid
1% acetic acid (based on weight of fabric)
2 gallons water

If more water is required to properly cover the cloth, increase the amounts proportionally.

Following the mordant bath, the cloth is rinsed (cool water) and dried.

67

City, 28" x 30". A mounted batik panel. Orange and red tones were applied with successive dye baths on dull yellow cloth.

Mounting and Finishing

When the wax is removed and the color set, the batik can be finished or mounted in a number of different ways. For wall hangings, the top and bottom of the piece can be stitched to form an opening through which a dowel rod can be inserted. To do this:

1. Be certain the raw edges are cut on a straight thread; correct, if necessary.

2. Stitch the raw edge down 1/4-1/2 inch, toward the back, top and bottom.

3. Pin the stitched edge down about 1 inch, measure evenly, stitch in place, leaving the ends open.

4. Insert 3/8 or 1/2 inch dowel rods through the top and bottom openings.

5. Attach small screw eyes through the ends of the top dowel rod for mounting.

For smaller pieces, it is sometimes preferable to mount them on stretcher frames, in a manner similar to mounting a canvas. If the batik is to be used on a wall, stretch and tack a lining cloth to the frame first, then stretch and tack the batik cloth over the protective lining.

If the frame is to be fitted over a light source, the lining is unnecessary. However, to protect the batik cloth from the rough corner edges of the stretcher frame, carefully cover the corners with masking tape, prior to tacking the batik.

Large pieces, designed for permanent installation in buildings, must be treated individually. Usually, some outer protection will be required and should be considered when the installation is planned. Glass or Plexiglass is often used. Sometimes it is necessary to attach or pin the batik cloth between two sheets of Plexiglass if fluorescent lighting is used from behind.

In regard to lighting, there is no doubt that it sometimes greatly enhances the color quality. However, the amount of light is important: too much light seems to weaken the color intensity. Careful planning is important in this type of installation. It is not recommended that a batik, or any dyed cloth, be permanently installed in a window.

Variations on the Batik Process

Starch Paste Resists

Resist techniques on textiles using starch paste solutions instead of hot wax, have been known for centuries in Africa, especially Nigeria, where the process is known as "adire eleko". These methods are of interest to the contemporary artist-craftsman, since they offer an intriguing variation to the hot wax resist and expand the range of surface and color effects achieved on cloth.

The resist is made by combining different flours and starches with water and cooking them until a clear paste solution is formed. A simple recipe which can be used for making samples to explore the technique is as follows: dissolve 3 tablespoons flour in 1 cup cold water, heat over a double boiler until clear, stirring constantly. A more satisfactory paste can be made with:

1 tablespoon corn starch
1 tablespoon white flour
1 tablespoon rice flour
1 tablespoon laundry starch (powdered)
½ teaspoon alum

Dissolve the flours and starches thoroughly in 1 cup cold water. Heat over a double boiler, stirring constantly, until the mixture becomes clear. Additional water is added in small amounts and stirred in, until the proper consistency is achieved. The mixture should be semitransparent and thick but still flow from the spoon, similar to honey. At this point the alum is added to the mixture.

The paste is applied to the cloth while warm, with the fabric either placed on a flat table or tacked lightly to a frame. Brushes of all sizes can be used, as well as flat wood sticks, palette knives, rollers or syringes. The paste is heavy and applied in a slow, deliberate manner. As the paste dries the cloth will pucker slightly. On most fabrics, the resist will not seep through evenly to the reverse side, but forms a layer on the top surface about 1/8 inch thick. When partially dry the surface can be broken by scratching or scraping into it with blunt tools.

Before the dyes are applied, the resist must be allowed to harden and dry completely. This takes from two to three days, depending on humidity. The resist will not hold up unless it has dried.

The cloth can be placed in a bath for dyeing but this is often not practical, since the areas coated with resist should not touch. It should be remembered also, that unless the paste was applied to both sides of the fabric, the resist will not be complete, and the dye will penetrate unevenly into the fibers from the reverse side. This is not necessarily a disadvantage, however, since very effective surface qualities can result.

On large sections of fabric, the dyes or dye pastes are best applied by brushes, sponges or paint rollers. As in batik, the dyes used should have an affinity for the cloth fiber. The correct procedure for fixing the dye should be followed.

When the dyes have been set, the cloth is placed in cold water for several minutes until the paste becomes soft. With the cloth spread out flat, the paste is scraped off using a plastic windshield scraper or spatula. When the paste is removed, the cloth can be ironed and the procedure of applying the paste and the dye can be repeated. It is also possible to utilize these effects as backgrounds for more detailed work with hot wax as the resist.

Cold Wax Emulsions

Cold wax emulsions, used as a resist on cloth are completely safe, since no heat is required. They can be applied directly from the container with sturdy brushes or flat wood sticks. Small squeegees of heavy cardboard or plastic are also effective tools.

The blocking-in of large shapes or patterns is fairly easy to control, but since these emulsions are quite thick in consistency, it is not possible to work with the freedom and spontaneity of the hot wax resist. In this respect, cold wax emulsions are similar to the starch paste resists, more suited to strong, bold images rather than delicate, linear effects. When the emulsion has dried completely, the surface can be broken by slightly folding or bending the cloth so that dye can penetrate into the cracks.

In applying the dyes, the use of the sponge, brush, or paint roller is preferable to the dyebath, so that excessive handling or crushing of the cloth is avoided. When the dyes have dried, the cold wax emulsion is removed in the same manner as the hot wax formula, by ironing between newspapers and, if necessary, soaking in solvent.

Polymer Emulsions

New products are available which can be used effectively as resists on cloth. These are clear, free-flowing polymer emulsions having a viscosity similar to light honey. No heat is necessary; the material is squeezed from the container spout directly onto the cloth, resulting in an effect somewhat similar to hot wax flowing from the tjanting tool. Used in this manner, it is ideal for linear designs on fine to medium weight fabrics. Also, it presents a safe, practical means of introducing young students to the batik process.

This material is easy to use. It is applied to the cloth directly from the container and is not difficult to control. A few minutes after application,

70

the resist soaks through to the under side of the fabric and seems to set. The cloth should be kept flat until the setting occurs, since any tilting could cause displacement of the resist. After setting, the fabric is placed in a hot (near boiling) dye bath. On contact with the hot liquid, the resist turns an opaque white. When the correct depth of dye color has been reached, the cloth is given a quick rinse in warm water and then immersed in cold water, where the resist dissolves when lightly rubbed, and can be washed away.

The polymer resist is practical for small sections of cloth, designed primarily with linear elements or small shapes. If the cloth is bunched too tightly in the dye bath, the resist will stick to itself. For blocking-in of large shapes, it is not as economical as wax and crackling effects cannot be obtained.

The major advantages of this resist over wax is that simmering hot dye baths can be used, giving better color fastness without steaming. Also, the emulsion needs no heating or prior preparation before using.

Seated Lady and *Acrobats.* These stuffed doll forms by Morag Benepe are enchanting figures in batik velvet garb.

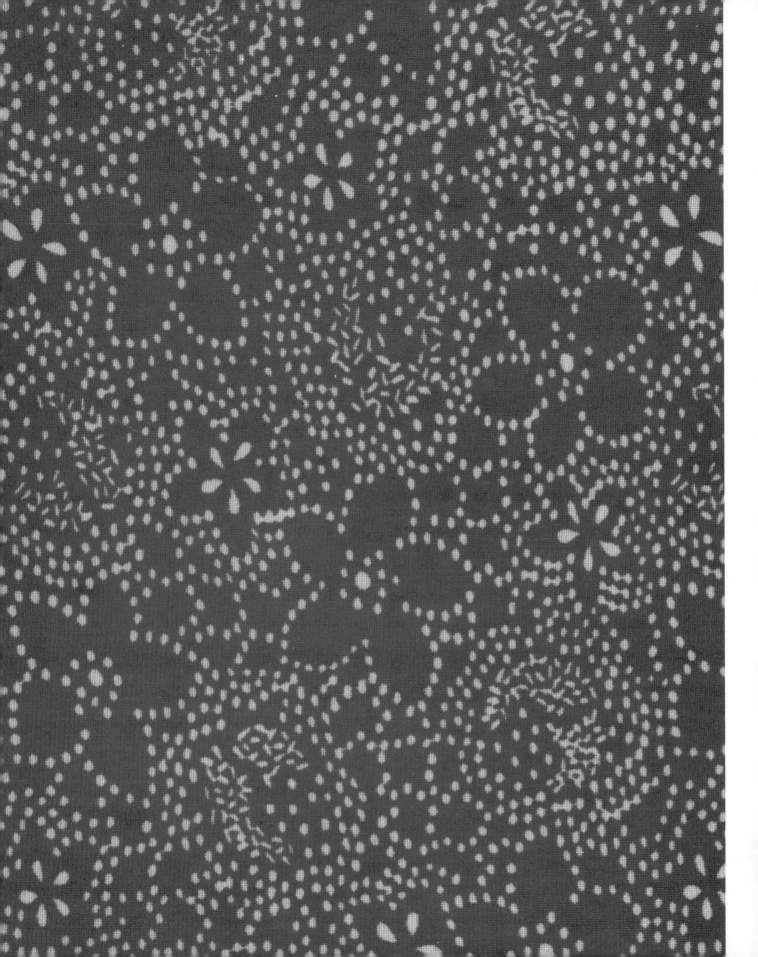

Tie Dye: History and Tradition

The traditions in the dye-resist processes involving the tying, knotting, binding or stitching of the fabric prior to dye immersion, are thought to be East Asian in origin. There are conflicting interpretations of evidence, however, which make a search for exact origins futile. There is reliable evidence of early knowledge of these processes in India, China, Japan, Java and Bali. In Africa, the application of reserve dye techniques indicates abundant usage on utilitarian objects as well as textiles. The design motifs from Africa are very different from those found in Asia. Some of the earliest textile fragments found, however, come from Peru, and it is believed that knowledge of these processes spread from Peru into Mexico and southwestern United States. Studies have indicated extensive applications of resist dye techniques on the North American continent, due to the widespread Peruvian influence, although there is greater continuity and more diverse application in the East Asian and Oriental civilizations.

Anthropologists have found that prototypes for simple resists are found in all primitive cultures. The bleaching action of the sun may have accidentally set off an awareness of a patterned surface obtained by a resist; from this realization, the concept of preparing material to resist coloration may have developed. Early tie and dye work on woven cloth was probably an adaptation of the ancient "ikat" technique, in which sections of the warp threads were bound off and tied prior to weaving. Ikat has been known for centuries in Eastern Indonesia, especially in Bali. From using the resist-dye processes on warp or unwoven threads, the concept of designating sections of finished cloth for reserve dyeing seems a natural development. For hundreds of years these peoples have produced textiles of remarkable delicacy of pattern and rich ornamental appeal.

Traditionally, the process consists of isolating and firmly tying off small portions of the cloth in a carefully regulated manner. These sections usually formed a geometric arrangement of circlets and narrow stripes and were bound with natural fiber cords to form a protection from the dye coloration. After the dye bath, the cords are removed and the pattern emerges.

The most elementary patterns in tie and dye are the small circlets so prevalent on textiles from India, Sudan, parts of Africa and Morocco. In spite of the technical simplicity of grasping and tying off a tiny segment

A contemporary fabric print adapted from the tie dye
design of an Indian sari.

73

of the cloth, many variations are possible. Large portions of the fabric can be reserved by incorporating specialized folding methods along with the binding. Circles, squares and other geometric shapes can be gathered so that the flow of the folds converge at one point, with firm ties placed at intervals.

In the sewing or "tritik" process, prevalent in African textiles, a long, sturdy thread is stitched into the fabric along a predetermined line direction . . . straight, wavy, zigzag, etc. The cord is then pulled taut so that the cloth gathers. When the fabric is tightly bunched up along the line of the cord, it is tied off, forming the resist. The dye cannot penetrate into the tightly enclosed gathers close to the cord.

All of these resist techniques have been known and practiced for centuries in the villages of India, especially in small centers close to large cities. A study of these fabrics is an introduction to the creative work of countless generations; cloth fragments have been found which go back 5,000 years. This folk or village tradition in Indian textiles reflected an expert knowledge of dyes. The saris, flared skirts, and head scarves, embellished with tie dyed motifs, were in a range of brilliant colors, each hue associated with a symbolic meaning based on local customs and religious ritual. The images were geometric or highly stylized interpretations of familiar myths.

Detail of a woven blanket from Indonesia in the "Ikat" or dyed warp technique. Before the cloth is woven, sections of the warp forming the pattern were carefully bound as a protection from the dye. After weaving, the resulting pattern appears blurred or slightly irregular.

Indian tie dye on silk. The small dots are bound with co‹ before dyeing. When the cords are removed the dots appe‹ white on a red background. In the center black dye w‹ brushed over some of the do‹

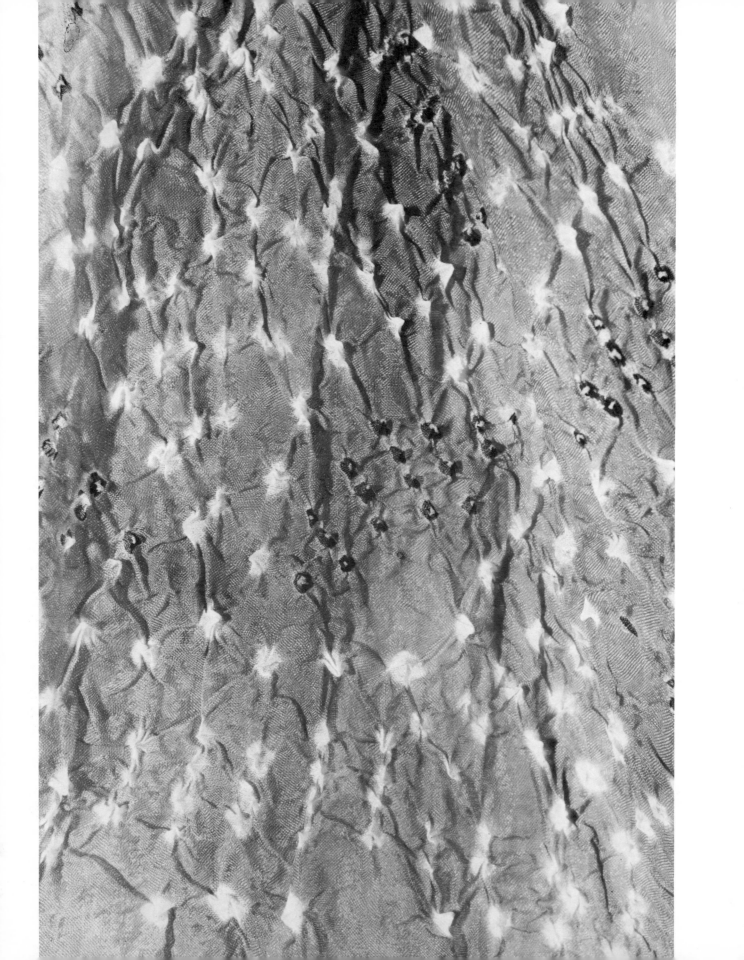

As in all traditional folk art, the degree of technical skill was amazing. The craftsmen were very carefully trained, often from childhood, in methods of working which were passed on from generation to generation. These were time-consuming skills, evident in the manner of preparing the thousands of tiny segments of cloth, all of which had to be carefully gathered and tied.

As in all folk crafts, industrialization has resulted in a breaking down of established traditions which have been practiced for centuries. In the textile crafts, this has meant a loss of indigenous design quality, as well as an impoverishment of the kinds of purposeful creative activity which are a wholesome and necessary part of personal and communal life.

The illustrations on these two pages show Indian tie dye on silk. A controlled pattern of circular lines forming an all-over floral motif. The crimped or creased surface is a distinctive quality of traditional tie dye work.

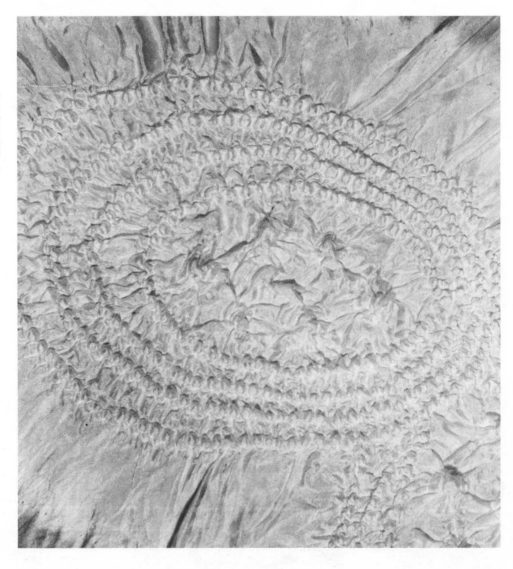

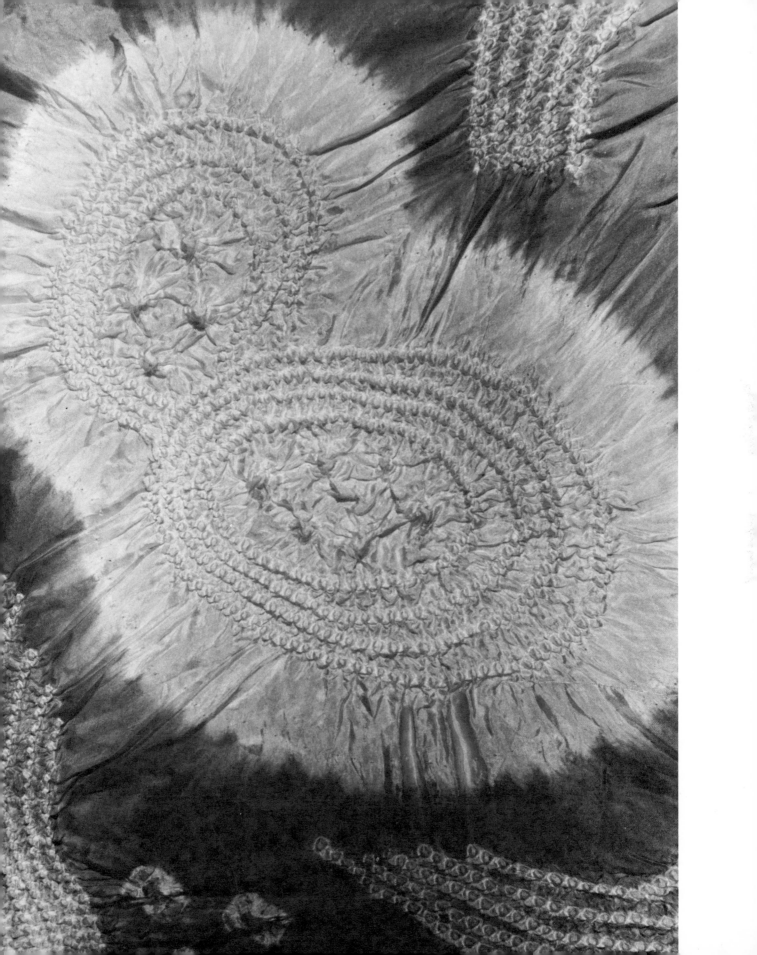

Indian tie dye on silk. This highly controlled pattern of a flower border and diagonal rows in the background was probably made by pressing the damp cloth onto a wooden block with raised prongs defining the design. The ties are made using these prongs as a guide.

Designing in Tie Resist Techniques

The tie resist techniques described offer unique opportunities for a kind of color exploration attuned to the discovery of the relationship between the planned and the accidental. In some ways, the visual effects are closely related to the qualities of free watercolor painting, especially where transparencies through over-dyeing occur. There can also be a distinct graphic quality.

The controls, obtained from the placement of the pleats, stitches and ties, can never be thought of as an absolute means of predetermining the final visual result. It is suggested that the beginner try out the techniques described on small pieces of fabric, to be kept as references for future work on larger panels, realizing that there are too many variables for exact duplication. Changes in weight and size of the fabric, in the fiber content, in manner of pleating, in tightness of the bind, in the temperature and timing of the dye bath—all of these, and more, imply a variation in the resulting image.

There are, however, certain aspects of these techniques which can be planned, and a basic familiarity with these is essential for blocking out placement and direction of shapes on larger pieces. The various methods of pleating are consistent in determining stripe directions: vertical, horizontal, diagonal, chevron, or squared. With the stitching and clamping methods, it is possible to control the placement and definition of both large and small shapes. The tritik technique is especially appropriate for those whose work temperament is inclined toward a more logical, predetermined surface rhythm.

It would not be wise for the beginner to settle too quickly into one particular mode of working or to give in so completely to the accidental effects which occur that all sense of planning is lost. The rewards of working in these processes come from learning to use the unpredictable effects to build more inventive design solutions. There is so much that can be discovered only by experimenting with an open awareness of "trial and error" possibilities. Often, an accidental effect can become the beginning of a new idea that will result in an increased sense of personal involvement. Working in these techniques over a long period of time gives the craftsman a deep understanding of the curious sense of balance between the planned and the unpredictable.

A contemporary tie dye by Carter Smith. Reds, oranges, green, and black were used in this vibrant wall hanging, 90" x 36".

These ancient techniques offer countless ideas which the inventive contemporary craftsman can utilize in many different ways. Some elementary practice is usually all that is required to become familiar with the method by which the effects are achieved and to observe and build on the resulting pattern image.

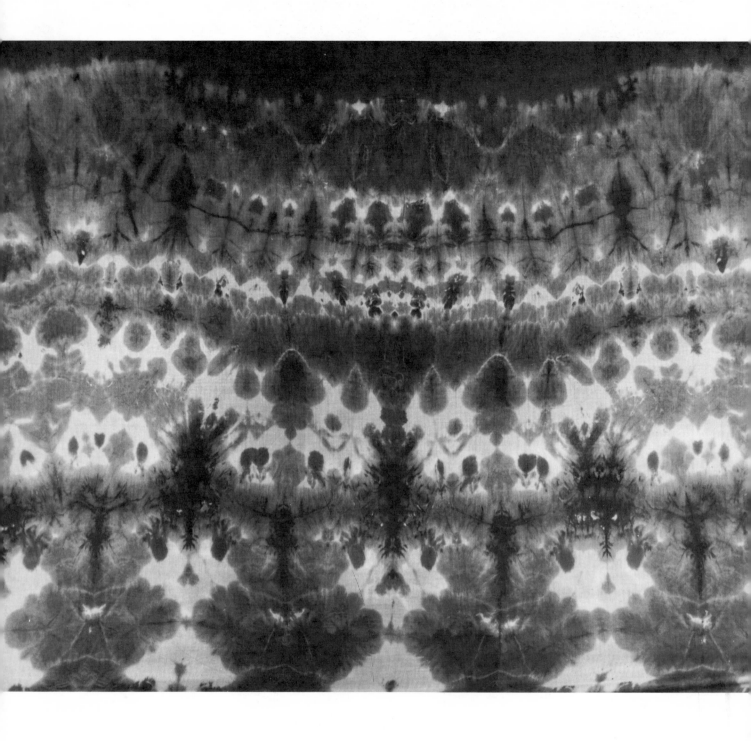

In this section of a large panel in cotton muslin, the patterned
surface results from random pleating, twisting and tying.
Direct dyes were used in brilliant yellows and blue.

82

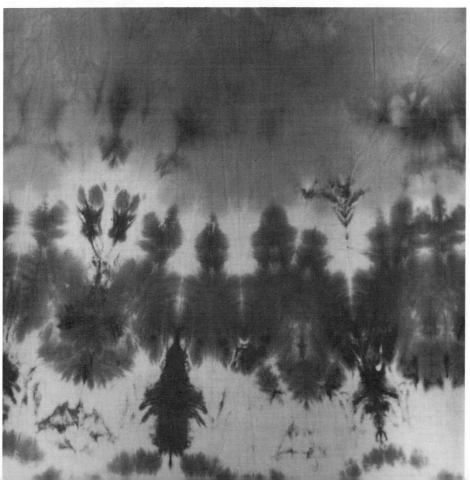

Resist Dye Process: Technical Notes

The Cloth

Many different kinds of cloth are suitable for resist dye techniques. Fine to medium weight cotton, viscose rayon, or silk, will be appropriate for all the processes described and are especially recommended for beginners. Heavier weight cottons, as well as woolens, can also be used with some technical modifications. When purchasing cloth, be certain of fiber content and avoid cloth that has been treated with a soil repellant or crease resistant finish.

The fabric should be cut as evenly as possible from selvage to selvage. If a cut edge is irregular, pick up a thread with a blunt needle and pull it out so that a slight pucker is made along the entire width of the cloth. This puckered line can be used as a guide in cutting. It is especially important that all of the edges be aligned when working in the folding and pleating methods. If a large panel is designed with several variations in folding and over-dyeing, it is suggested that raw edges be hemmed first.

Before beginning, wash the cloth in hot soapy water, allow to dry, and iron flat.

Binding and Tying

Different kinds of cord and thread will be suitable for tying; choices should be made by considering the type of cloth used as well as the kind of resist that is wanted. Strength is an important factor. The material should not break easily under pressure of the ties.

On fine fabrics, thin cords, such as buttonhole twine or carpet thread, are excellent and can be used on silk, cotton lawn, thin muslin and viscose rayon. Heavier cords, sold for package wrapping, can be used on medium weight cloth. Raffia is also a fine material for binding and tying, especially effective on medium to heavy weight fabric. Raffia will withstand absorption by the dye liquid, making for a very strong resist. Wide, sturdy rubber bands can be used when appropriate, as well as one-fourth inch rayon or nylon elastic, sold by the yard. Water-repellant cloth can be cut into one-half inch strips and used for tying; some craftsmen have used nylon fish line for bindings on thin cloth.

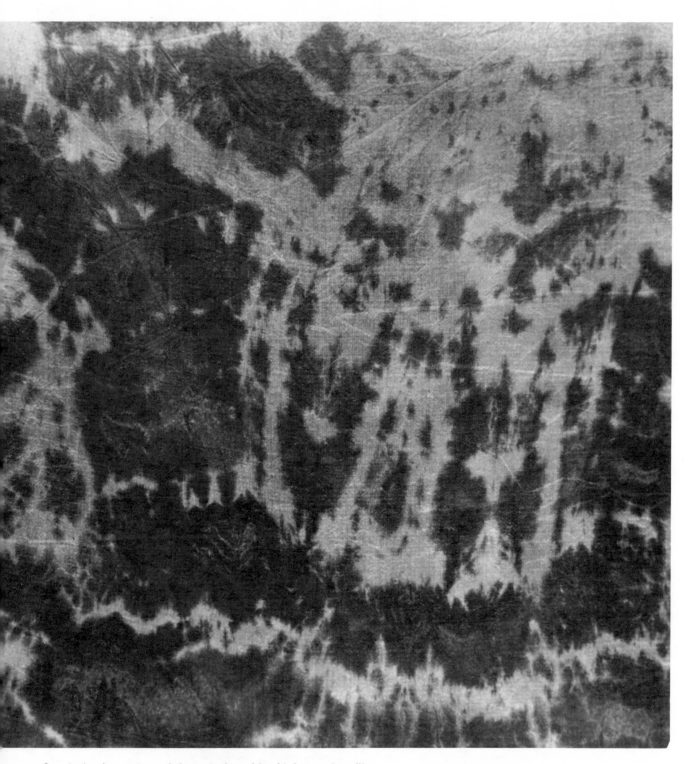

Sample showing random twisting and tying, with acid dyes used on silk.

The particular way that the cords are tied and the tightness of the bind determine the character of the resist. The cord must be wound very firmly if the dye coloration is to be kept out. If the cloth is slightly dampened, the ties can be made much tighter. Partial dampening can be achieved efficiently by spraying soft water (Calgon) onto each section. Use a bottle with a push-spray top, as those used originally for household cleaning solutions. Damp cloth will compress readily, allowing for a much firmer resist than can be obtained on dry fabric.

The cord can be put on in different ways to produce a variety of resulting patterns. When the cord is bound around the fabric in a very solid manner, closely filling the space, the dye will not penetrate into the cloth. The resist can be strengthened by an additional layer of cord or raffia. When the cord is bound around the fabric in a widely-spaced, cross-over manner, the result will be a partial resist. Some dye will penetrate into the cloth, forming an irregular stripe pattern. Often, when the cord is tied in this lattice manner, a distinct line appears in the resist image, imparting a very graphic quality.

Regardless of the manner in which the cord is bound, it must be fastened off securely if it is to hold in the dye bath. A tight double knot is best. If, after binding, one of the end cords has become too short for proper tying, attach a new length of cord by winding it several times around the former end (from the same direction) until it is tight and can be tied with the longer end.

Cutting the cords after dyeing requires unusual care because the cloth can be easily damaged. Usually it is possible to pull the knot away from the bound area and insert one of the scissor points. Do not use scissors which are too sharply pointed. After cutting, the cord is wound off, with additional clipping sometimes necessary. The cord can be saved, to be used again later.

Rubber bands are used in much the same manner as cords, except that their use is limited to areas of the cloth that can be reached within the grasp of the hand. They are stretched while winding and must be very sturdy or they will snap. Remove the rubber bands by any means that seems appropriate, pulling away or clipping.

The best time to remove bindings is while the cloth is still somewhat damp, about an hour away from completely drying. Once removed, the cloth should then be immediately ironed.

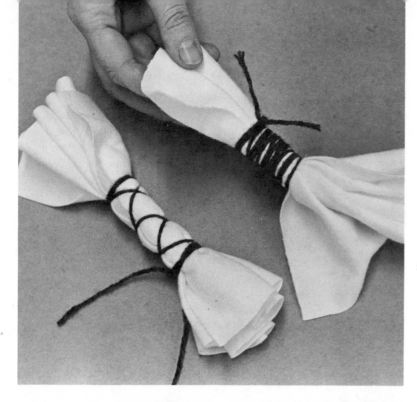

Samples with different methods of tying.

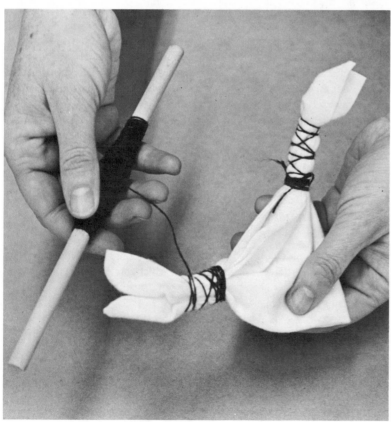

A squared cloth sample, folded into a triangle and tied at two corners. The cord is wrapped on a dowel stick.

Use of Dyes in Tie Resist Techniques

General information about different kinds of dyes available should be reviewed, since it is important to use a dye with an affinity for the cloth fiber. In tie resist dyeing, the cloth is immersed in the dye bath for a relatively short period of time, usually about five to ten minutes. There can be instances, however, when one minute is sufficient (on thin silk) or when an hour or more might be necessary (on heavy wool) to obtain the required depth of color. Some caution is needed, since it is possible to destroy the subtleties of the resist by allowing the fabric to remain in the dye bath for too long a time. The bath can be lukewarm or hot, depending on the particular requirements of the dye. In preparing the dye bath, the objective is for a strong concentration which will provide the appropriate strength of color in as short a time as possible.

There are so many constantly changing considerations in tie resist dyeing, it does not seem practical to try to work with exact proportions. A solution is to make a concentrated mixture of three-fourths to one teaspoon dye to one pint of water and make a test on a small piece of the cloth, noting the temperature of the bath as well as the time. Additional water or dye can be added as the sample indicates. A proportionate amount of the exhaust agent should also be added. Since the solution is so strong, the dye is seldom exhausted after one bath; it can be reused at a later time or mixed with another color.

Partial Dyeing. It is not necessary that the entire fabric be placed in the dye bath. The cloth can be designed with several stripes or shapes of different colors. Horizontal, vertical, chevron stripes, as well as folded and bound shapes, can be dyed as separate units. Large sections of multicolor striping can serve as a background for smaller, more detailed resist patterns.

Prior to placing the section in the dye bath, check the boundaries on each side of the color to be certain they are securely tied off. Since each color is dyed separately, care in handling is essential when removing the individually dyed sections from the bath. Plastic bags, sold on a roll in grocery stores, are excellent for protecting the remaining areas of the cloth from accidental spotting. While this method of dyeing is somewhat time-consuming, it offers numerous possibilities for inventive color exploration.

Over-dyeing. Much of the interest and variety in resist dyeing comes from over-dyeing: that is, recoloring cloth which has been previously dyed. Usually, the fabric is folded again, then bound, stitched, or clamped to form a new resist image. A basic familiarity with color-mixing principles is important when over-dyeing so that the second color chosen will effectively recolor the first. While there are no exact rules, a light or bright color is usually applied first, to be over-dyed with another color of the same value or one that is more intense or darker.

If the first color is	over-dyed with	will produce
yellow	red	orange
	blue	green
	purple	brown
red (medium)	yellow	orange
	blue	purple
	green	brown
blue (medium)	yellow	green
	red	purple
	orange	brown

This guide is very generalized, dealing only with primary colors. Secondary colors in over-dyeing result in hundreds of variations and would be impossible to categorize.

Sample showing one corner of the triangle dipped into the dye bath. Other colors can be used on the remaining corners.

Tie dye on cotton batiste. The sections of the dress were first cut from a simple pattern. After the folding, tying, and dyeing processes were completed the pieces were sewn together. (Sarah Tobin)

90

Mixing Dye Colors. After working with the dyes for a brief time, the effects of color mixing will be noticed. Often, when two dye colors are mixed together to produce a new color (e.g. green obtained by mixing yellow and blue) there will be a natural separation occurring on the cloth at places under the binding ties. The dyes penetrate the fibers at different rates and the more active color will extend out of the mixture into the gathered, folded or tied areas of the fabric. These effects can often be predicted and can be utilized to great advantage in tie dye work.

Random Effects

There are many ways of treating the cloth to produce random effects on the overall surface of the fabric. Preplanning is at a minimum with these methods; in fact, the attempt to plan is discouraged by the very nature of the procedures. These techniques are, however, an excellent introduction to tie dye processes because they encourage spontaneous experimentation in handling and binding the cloth. In addition, they provide opportunities to become familiar with the dyes, both in color usage and in application.

The results, although unpredictable, are often very effective visually and should be evaluated as possibilities for additional work in folding, tying, tritik and related techniques. The following suggestions will be most suited to thin fabrics, about 36 inches wide and 1½ yards long, or smaller.

1. Spread the cloth flat on a table surface. Grasp a section of the fabric with one hand. While holding the bunched up cloth, wrap cord tightly around the area in a criss-cross manner. Without tying off the cord, grasp another section nearby and tie in the same manner. Continue this until the entire surface of the cloth has been bunched up and tied. The cloth can be sprayed lightly to dampen and additional ties can be made. The cloth can be dyed as follows:

   a. Dye in one color, a light value. When dry, additional ties can be made throughout the cloth. Then dye again in a more intense bath of the same color.

   b. Dye in one color. When dry, make additional ties and dye again in a new color.

   c. Dip the sections in several different colors. When dry, make additional ties and dye again in a new color.

   d. After dyeing according to method a or b, the fabric can be untied, ironed, and the entire process of bunching and tying can be repeated with a different placement. The fabric is again dyed.

2. Fold the cloth in half and make a series of unmeasured vertical pleats or gathers. Holding one end firmly, begin twisting the entire length of the fabric with the other hand. On lengths of over a yard it is more practical to clamp down one end or have another person hold it while the twisting is being done. As the twisting becomes very tight, the cloth will seem to coil on itself. Bring the two ends together, allowing the coils to

91

In this wall hanging by Carter Smith, several tie dye techniques are utilized in the circular motif centered in a background of brilliant red.

Tying sections of cloth, gathered at random.

form naturally. Tie the two ends together first, and then place a few additional ties around the coils. The cloth can be dyed in any of the methods suggested above.

3. Tie objects into the cloth in a random placement. Dowel rod pieces of different lengths are especially effective in producing circular patterns in the cloth. Insert the piece of doweling into the cloth and smooth the fabric around it from the point to the base. As the cloth gathers toward the base of the rod, try to distribute the bulk evenly. Bind first at the base, while holding the gathers firmly. Then place additional ties at intervals along the dowel piece, either as a solid bind or in a criss-cross manner. Repeat this procedure throughout the cloth, using the different lengths of doweling.

The fabric can be dyed in any of the previously suggested methods. Procedure c as listed above will be especially useful, resulting in very rich over-dye effects in the circular patterns.

Different kinds of objects can be tied into the cloth, as well, each resulting in a distinctive pattern image. Pieces of wood lattice stripping, wood or plastic thread spools, buttons, and washers are all suitable.

92

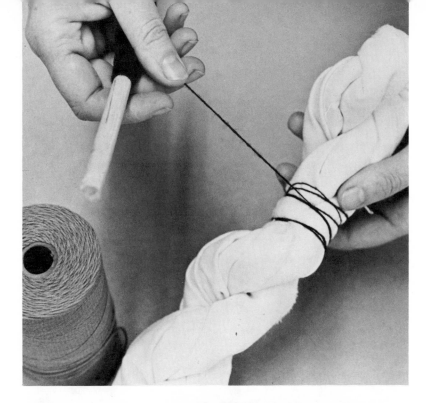

A twisted and coiled length of cloth is tied at intervals.

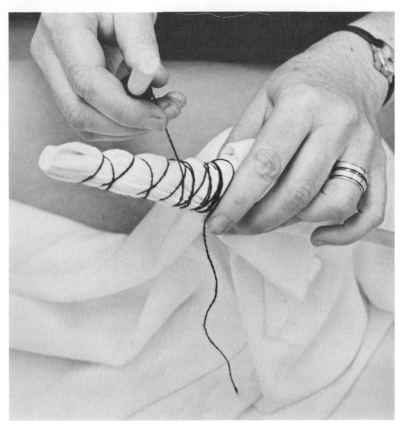

A dowel stick is tied into the cloth.

This design was produced by dowel sticks tied at random into the cloth.

Methods of Folding

On long sections of cloth, the basic fold technique is an accordian-like type of pleating extending from one end of the fabric to the other. This pleating, combined with additional folds and bindings, will result in many effective patterns. The width of each pleat, as well as the number of pleats that can be formed, will be determined by the weight of the fabric. A thin, soft fabric can be folded many times, while a heavier fabric will naturally be more suited to fewer pleats. Fine cloth can be folded in half first and then formed into the pleats.

It is possible to measure out each pleat for precision in placement. To do this, the cloth is placed on a flat table surface or on the floor while the pleats are measured with a yardstick and marked with a pencil. As each pleat is formed it is held in place with pins or paper clamps, until all of the pleating is completed.

It is not necessary that all of the pleats be of the same width. Variations in spacing can occur at any time. For example, wide pleats can be placed at the center, gradually becoming narrower toward the selvages of the fabric. Or, just the reverse can be planned, with the wide pleats at the edges and a gradual narrowing at the center. The procedure for measuring and pinning is the same. After the initial lengthwise pleating is completed, the fabric can be tied at intervals and dyed.

94

Image formed by controlled pleating and tying.

Variations in folding techniques occur when, in addition to the lengthwise pleating, more folding is done along the pleated section. These techniques are most effective on thin fabric or small pieces. If a full width fabric is used, the spacing of the pleats is usually wider—perhaps four or five inches apart—than the spacing on a narrow length of cloth.

On a rectangular shaped piece of cloth, the lengthwise folds or pleats are made first and pinned into place. Then, additional pleating or folding can be done in a number of different ways.

1. The pleated length of cloth, taken as a whole, is folded from one end to the other in a series of evenly spaced pleats. The resulting packet of cloth is then tied in the center. Since many layers of cloth are in the bundle, the ties must be very firmly made. Raffia or wide rubber bands would be excellent. If the cloth is damp, a tighter bind can be made. Prior to dyeing, pull apart the exposed pleat edges to allow the dye to be evenly absorbed. The dyeing can be done as follows:

   a. The entire bundle can be dyed one color.

   b. One end of the bundle is dyed one color, the other end in another color.

   c. To introduce additional variation in pattern and color, after the initial dyeing, the entire folding and tying procedure can be repeated on a slightly different alignment. The second dyeing method can be either a or b, as listed above.

2. Fold the cloth in four or six pleats lengthwise. One end of the pleated cloth, taken as a whole, is folded from one of the corners diagonally over to the opposite side, forming a triangle. This diagonal folding is alternately repeated for the remaining length of the cloth. Work on a large table surface so the fabric can be conveniently turned for each fold. The resulting packet will be triangular in shape. Using rubber bands or raffia, bind the two corners following the long side of the triangle. This method will produce a diamond shaped pattern, the number of points determined by the number of lengthwise folds. Dye in the methods described above.

3. For a chevron stripe or zigzag effect, fold the cloth in half and lightly mark a series of diagonal lines from the center fold down to the selvage sides. The lines should be parallel, about two-four inches wide. Carefully form pleats along the lines, holding with pins whenever necessary. The cloth will form into a long, narrow strip. Tie at various intervals, and dye. When rinsed and partially dry, add additional ties and dye a second color. For two chevron stripes, fold-pleat the cloth in four sections.

◀

Image formed by controlled pleating and tying.

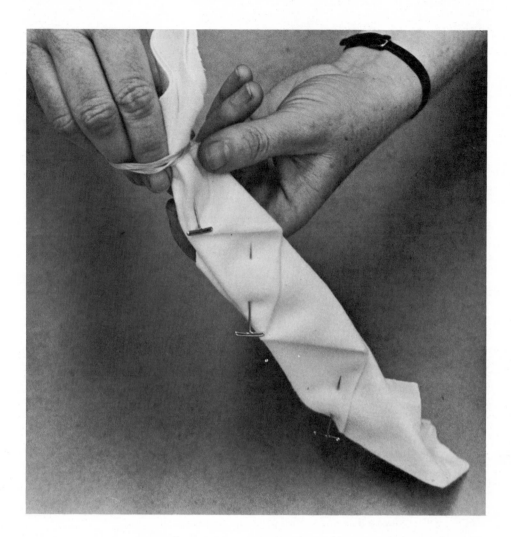

Folding and tying procedure for chevron stripe.

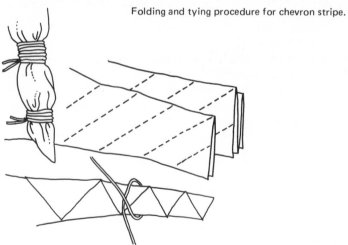

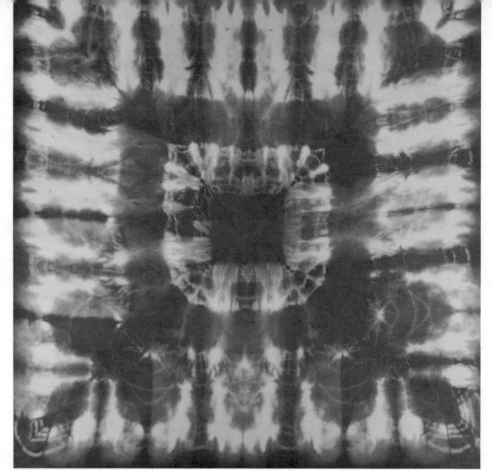

Patterns on square sections of cloth.

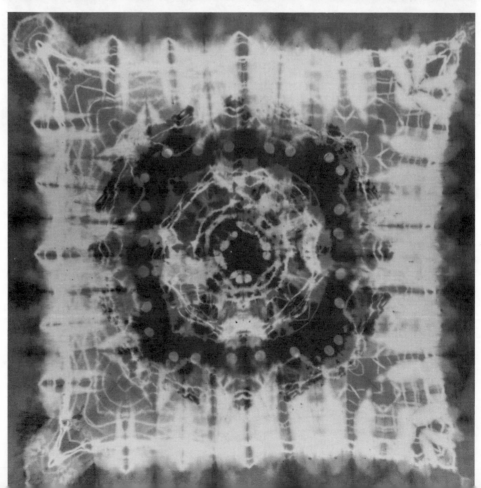

Detail of pattern of a folded
and tied square cloth.

Methods of Folding Square Sections of Cloth

A square section of cloth lends itself to techniques of folding which
utilize the four even sides of the cloth; the resulting pattern is based on
the square format. Although all of the folding methods suggested for rectangular sections of fabric can be used on squares, there are several techniques of folding which are especially appropriate for this shape. Again,
where measuring and marking is called for, it should be done with a yardstick and pencil. For some of the folds, it may be necessary to mark the
exact center of the square with a dot.

The following suggestions for folding utilize the square to advantage.

1. Bring one corner over to the opposite point, forming a triangle.
Fold in half, forming a smaller triangle. Starting with the longest side,
make three to five accordian type pleats toward the center point. Tie
and bind at several intervals. Dye in one or more colors.

2. Bring each corner in to touch the center dot, pin in place. A smaller
square shape will result. Fold this in half, with the point edges on the out-
side. Gather and tie at various intervals. Dye in one or more colors. Re-
align ties and dye again.

3. Fold the square in half and then in half again. Using this as the basis,
experiment with many different ways of gathering, folding and tying.

101

Tritik

Many kinds of strongly defined shapes can be dyed into the cloth using the tritik or sewing technique. It allows for a great deal of versatility and because of the control possible, a very personal kind of imagery can be developed by combining this method with the various folding, binding and clamping techniques. The stitches can be made on unfolded as well as folded cloth.

No real knowledge of sewing in the dressmaking sense is necessary, as these methods are extremely simple in themselves; the complexity comes about in the designing. Any fabric suitable for tie dye can be used, ranging from lightweight to heavy—although a more effective resist can be obtained on a lighter weight cloth. The size of the needle, the cord, and the length of the stitch will depend on what is appropriate to the type of fabric being used. Embroidery needles, long, sharp and with a large eye, are ideal for tritik. Ordinary sewing thread, doubled, is suitable for working on silk and thin cottons. On medium to heavy weight fabric, use carpet or buttonhole cord. The size of the cord is not as important as its strength; if it breaks easily do not use it.

The stitch most frequently used in tritik is called the running stitch: a consistent over and under passing of the needle through the cloth. The length of the stitch can vary from about ¼" to ½". A very sturdy knot should be made in the cord before beginning the stitching.

The basic procedure is to use the stitching to outline the shape, then gather or tightly pull up the threads and firmly tie off the ends to hold the gathers in place. The sewing can be done on a single thickness of cloth, or, where a symmetrical spacing is planned, the fabric is folded from edge to edge. The method of dyeing is similar to that used in the other resist techniques.

Before applying the tritik technique to large panels, several variations should be tried out on small lengths of cloth (¾-1 yard square) which can be kept as reference samples.

1. Stripes: a straight line of running stitches, gathered, tied and dyed, will produce a textured linear band in resist. Parallel rows of stitches will form an overall textural surface. Curved lines, as well as zigzag line formations can be stitched in this manner.

2. Shapes: specific shapes can be outlined in tritik to obtain a resist against the background. If a strong image is planned, it will be necessary to reinforce the shape outline by adding several additional, parallel rows of stitches.

3. Tucked pleats: make a pleat or tuck in the cloth about one to two inches deep. Pin in place and stitch along the base of the pleat with running stitches. Expand this idea to a series of parallel tucks, or tucks following curved, pointed or diagonal lines.

Samples showing various methods of stitching.

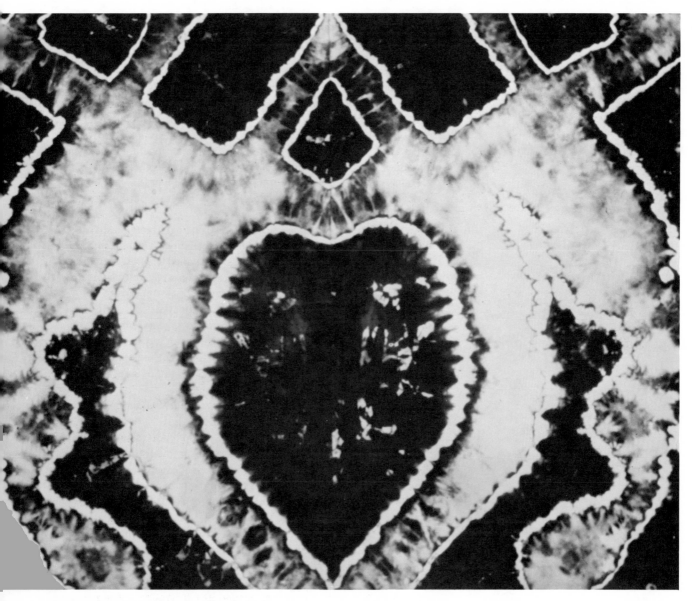

Detail of a wall hanging by Marion Clayden using
tritik and tying techniques on silk.

Using Solid Templates

A reinterpretation of a Japanese technique called "jamming" allows for the dyeing-in of very clearly defined shapes. The principle involved is that of tightly clamping several layers of cloth between two solid templates which form the resist, protecting the cloth from the dye. The templates can be of any shape and made of any material not affected by immersion in the liquid dye baths. Rigid sheet plastic, nonrusting metal, one-fourth inch plywood or masonite board can be used. Wood and hardboard can be cut on a jig or band saw without too much difficulty; the pieces should be sanded and coated with shellac for protection. Geometric shapes of 18 gauge copper are available from commercial suppliers. Galvanized washers of different sizes, purchased in hardware stores, can also be used as template resists.

A very sharp distinct resist can be made using rigid templates. The technique is best suited to fine or medium weight fabrics which can be tightly compressed; any fabric, however, properly handled, can be adapted to this method. When planning the design, it is important to remember that the more the fabric is folded with more layers of cloth between the clamps, the greater the chance of a hazy, indistinct resist. A fine fabric, such as China silk, can be pleated into from ten to twenty layers with clear results, while a medium to heavy weight cloth can only be pleated to form six to ten layers. Initial tests on small pieces of the material are helpful prior to planning the design. The fabric should be sprayed damp prior to clamping.

The clamps used must also be impervious to repeated dippings in dye liquid. Aluminum C type clamps are most practical. Although the aluminum clamp is about twice as expensive as the common castiron type, it is a necessity for serious work in this method. It is important that enough clamps be placed on the template to insure an adequate resist. The heavier the fabric and the larger the size of the template shape, the greater the number of clamps necessary. Small washers can usually be held with one clamp. Each clamp should be tightened as far as possible.

After clamping, the cloth sections on each side of the template can be refolded, bunched, tied or knotted in any number of different ways, depending on the character of the overall image. Templates can be used on undyed cloth, creating a white resist, or on cloth which has been previously dyed with stripes or other appropriate backgrounds. The template resist will be in the first color and the area surrounding it in the second color produced by the over-dye.

Wall hanging on satin using clamping techniques as well as pleating and tying methods.

104

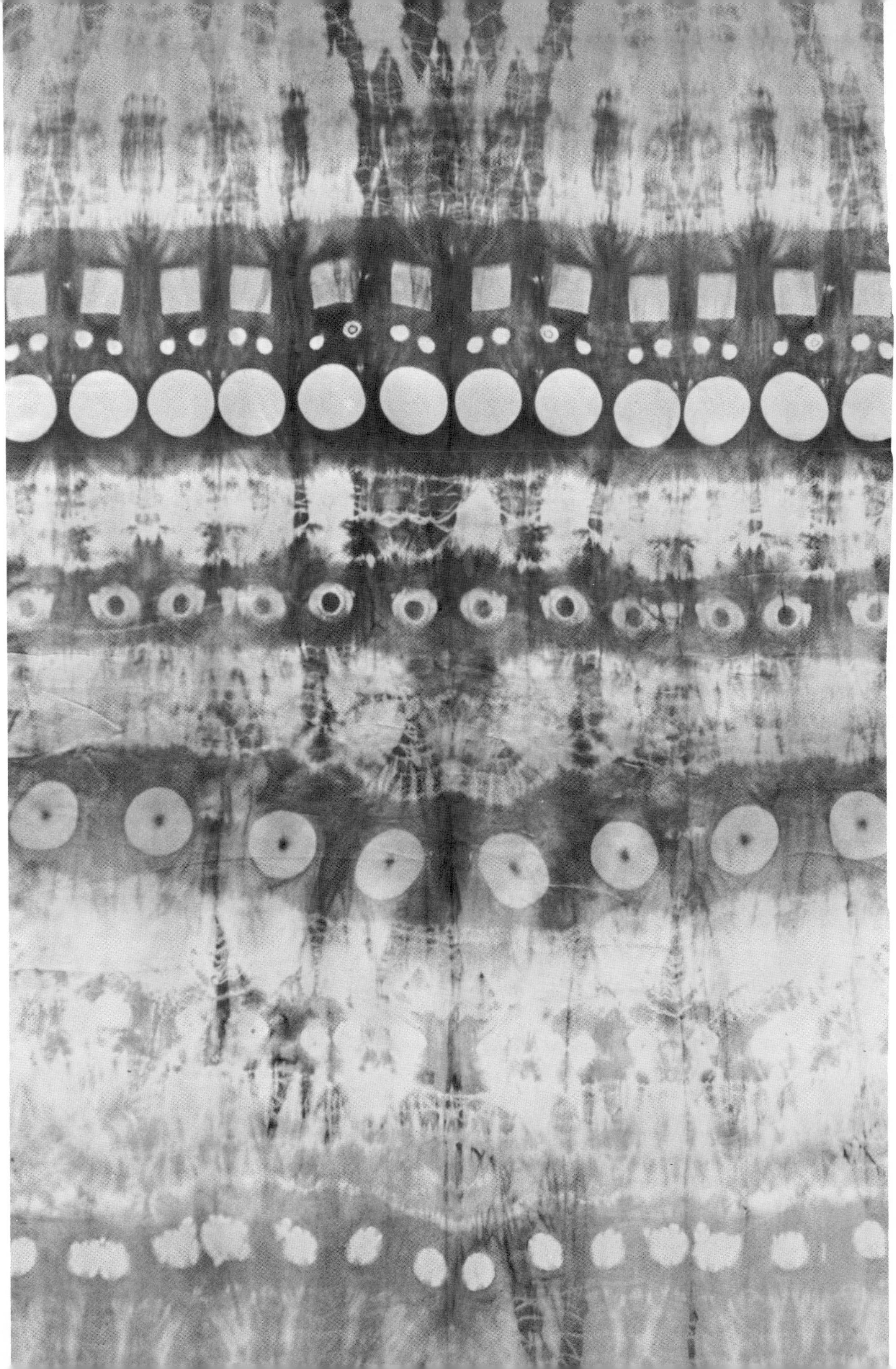

The dyeing procedure is similar to that of the other resist methods, but a somewhat larger vessel may be needed to accommodate the clamps. If the templates are used only in one section, protect the remaining cloth with a plastic bag. After the dye bath, place the fabric on newspaper for a time, rinse and allow to dry. When the cloth is almost dry, loosen the clamps and remove the templates and whatever other cords and bindings were used. Unfold the fabric and iron, first warm and then at the appropriate temperature for the cloth.

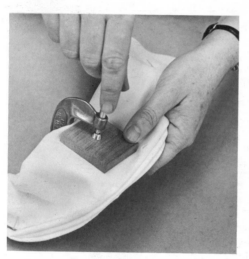

Clamping the pleated cloth between two wood blocks.

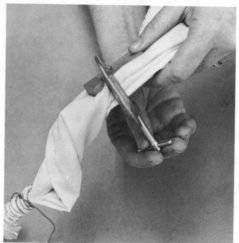

Clamped section placed in the dye bath. At left, a hand clamp holds the rim of a plastic bag which protects the rest of the cloth from dye splashes.

Wall hanging on cotton using discharge methods with pleating, clamping, and tying.

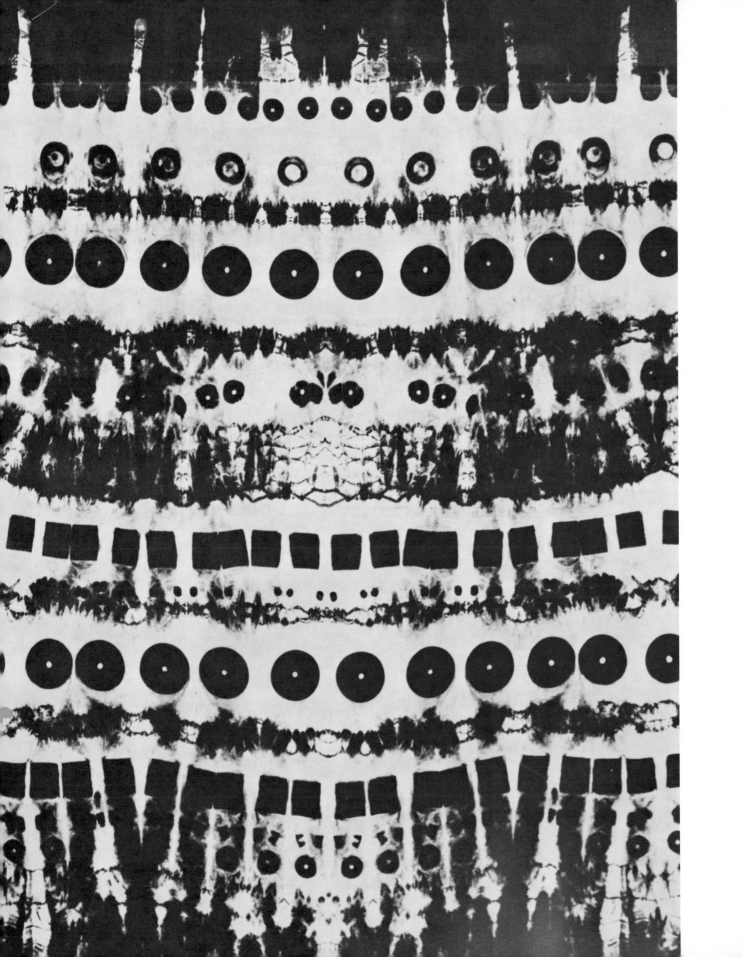

Discharge Dyeing

A variation on the standard tie and dye procedure, and one well worth exploring, is discharge dyeing. In these methods, the color is removed from the cloth, rather than added, with the bindings and ties serving to protect the original color of the fabric. All of the techniques described for use on white cloth can be utilized in discharge dyeing; the difference is that the fabric is a very dark or very intense color. In addition to folding and tying, sewing and clamping methods can be used successfully.

The color is removed by immersing the fabric in a chlorine bleach solution. When purchasing cloth for discharge dyeing, it is first necessary to test a small piece in a chlorine solution to be certain that the color will actually bleach out. Many commercially dyed fabrics are resistant to bleaching and cannot be used. Inexpensive cotton remnants are more likely to be satisfactory in this regard. If there is some rayon content in the cloth, the color may bleach out, but not to white. Black, for example, may bleach to orange or brown; dark blue may bleach to gray or pink. These results are impossible to predict in advance but can be most effectively used with these techniques. If suitable fabric cannot be purchased, it is possible to dye a length of cloth in the usual manner, rinse, dry, and then use it as a base for the discharge dye methods. A safe solution is:

> 1 part household bleach
> 2 parts water

Details of images resulting from discharge dyeing.

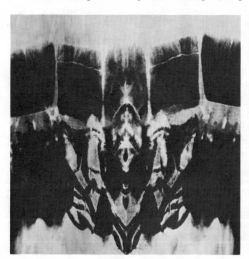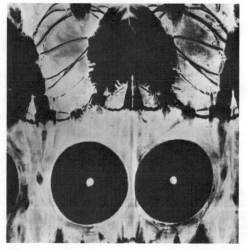

108

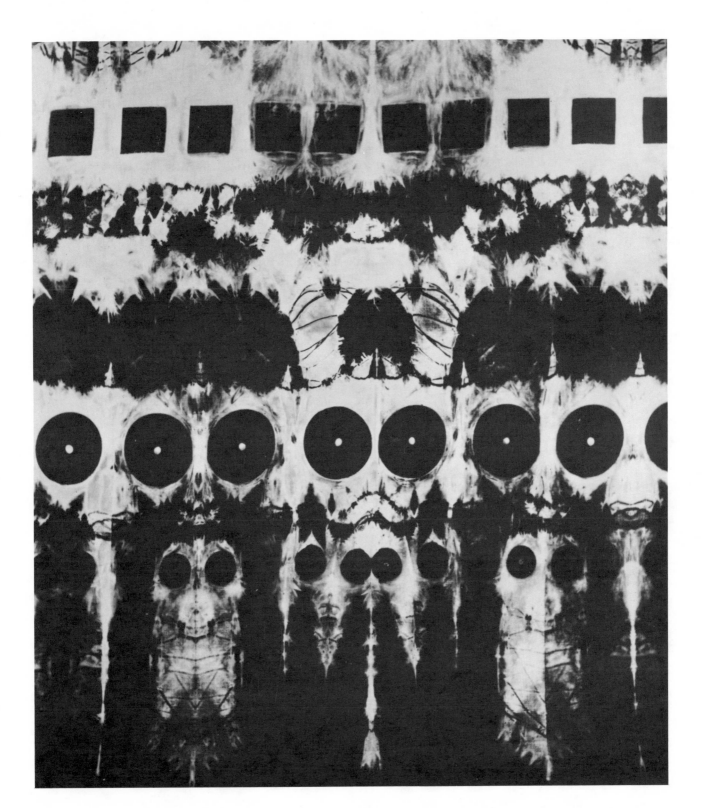

The bleaching action will be faster if a stronger mixture is used, but caution is necessary, since there is a possibility of damaging the fibers. The procedure is as follows:

1. Fold and tie the cloth in the usual manner.

2. Wet the cloth completely.

3. Immerse the fabric in the bleach solution. Wear rubber gloves and move the cloth about frequently. The bleaching action can be clearly observed.

4. When the proper amount of bleaching has occurred, remove the fabric and place it immediately in a rinse bath. After a few minutes, rinse again.

5. Wash the cloth with soap and hot water to completely remove every trace of the bleaching mixture. The addition of water softener to the last rinse will aid in removing the chlorine odor.

This work should be done in a well-ventilated area. Sometimes the chlorine fumes are irritating. Always wear rubber gloves; the bleach should not touch the skin in full strength.

Discharge dyeing offers many opportunities for inventive experimentation with the various methods of folding, tying, stitching, and clamping. The examples illustrated here, by Ruth Bilowus, show how rows of sewing machine stitches can delineate the shapes in the design, resulting in unique textural effects. In this technique the cloth is folded in half and then folded again. Two parallel rows of machine stitching trace around the design, while forming a channel between the layers of fabric tight enough to resist the bleach. When the stitching is completed, the cloth is placed first in water and then in a weak bleach solution to discharge the original color. Since the cloth is folded, the bleach will reach the outer layers first. It is necessary to work the solution into the cloth by squeezing and opening the layers. When the required bleaching has occurred the cloth is rinsed in the manner described above. After the fabric has dried the stitches are removed by carefully cutting the threads with a seam ripper.

Wall hanging by Ruth Bilowus using both machine stitching and clamping techniques to form the resist. The red taffeta was bleached to a light orange.

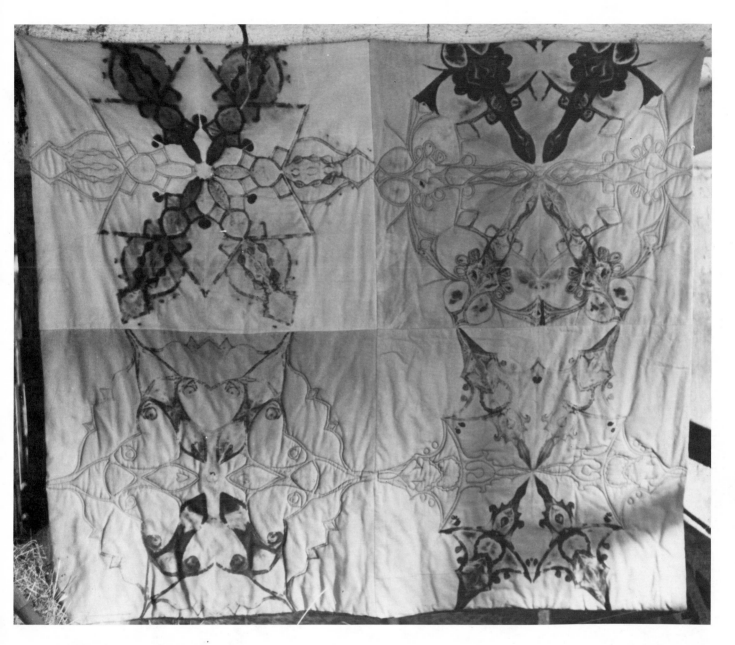

Parallel rows of machine stitching indicate the linear snow-
flake tracery pattern in this quilt by Ruth Bilowus. Some
portions of the original image were lost in the bleaching
but later redefined by machine quilting in a contrasting
color. The dark red cotton was bleached to off-white.

Detail of quilt.

With an understanding of the technical aspects of a medium, the first step has been taken. Understanding and doing, however, go hand in hand. Possibilities have been presented, but only by doing and, therefore, by actually using these possibilities, can individual confidence and creative growth occur. It is hoped that in addition to technical knowledge, the joy and challenge of working in batik and tie dye has been conveyed, as well.

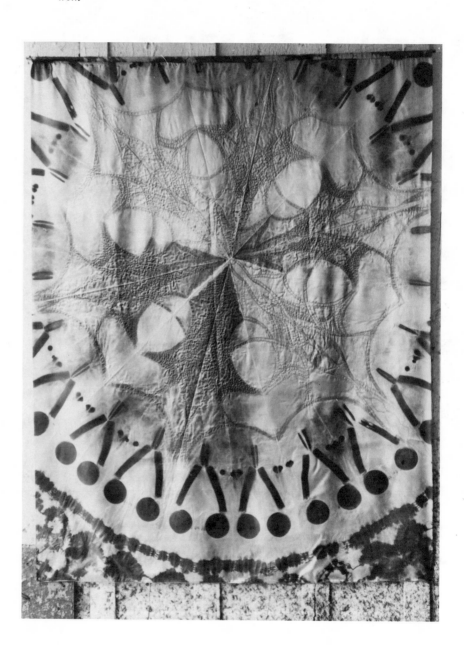

Glossary

Acid dyes   A group or class of dyes especially formulated for use on protein fibers, silk and wool.

Crackle   In batik, the fine, web-like network of lines over the surface of the cloth, caused by cracks made in the wax prior to dyeing.

Direct dyes   A group or class of dyes especially appropriate for use on cellulostic fibers, cotton, linen, and viscose rayon.

Discharge dyeing   Removing color from cloth using a bleach solution.

Dye bath   The proportionate mixture of dyestuff, water, and required additives necessary to achieve coloration on the cloth.

Ikat   A resist dye technique in which certain predetermined sections of the warp yarns are tightly bound as a protection from the dye. This is done prior to weaving.

Mordants   Chemical agents used to increase or promote dye absorption and fastness, required by most natural dyes.

Over-dyeing   Applying new dye coloration on cloth initially dyed in a different color.

Plangi   A Malaysian term referring to different types of tie dye techniques.

Resist   A substance (e.g. wax) or a method (e.g. tritik) which can be applied to protect predetermined portions of the cloth from dye penetration.

Solvent   A commercially prepared solution used to dissolve wax, or for various related cleaning purposes.

Templates   Pre-cut shapes, formed of solid, non porous material which can be used as resists when applied to the cloth with clamping methods.

Tjanting   A tool for applying wax to cloth, consisting of a reservoir to hold the hot wax, a spout through which the wax flows onto the fabric, and a handle.

Tjap   An Indonesian stamping tool used to apply intricate patterns of wax onto the cloth.

Tritik   A resist textile technique requiring the use of different stitches sewn into the cloth, which are gathered and fastened off to form a protection from the dye.

Wax formula   The proportionate combination of paraffin and beeswax (or soft industrial wax) used as a hot resist in the batik process.

Directory of Suppliers

Dyes

Aljo Manufacturing Co.
116 Prince Street
New York, New York 10012

direct, acid and basic dyes
dye paste mixture

Bachmeier & Company
154 Chambers Street
New York, New York 10007

direct, acid and basic dyes

W. Cushing & Company
Kennebunkport, Maine 04046

all-purpose dyes
(household dyes)

Dharma Trading Company
1952 University Avenue
Berkeley, California 94701

Procion^{TM} *dyes*

Fezandie & Sperrle
103 Lafayette Street
New York, New York 10013

direct and acid dyes

Keystone Aniline Company
321 North Loomis Street
Chicago, Illinois 60607

direct, acid and basic dyes

Pylam Products
95-10 218th Street
Queens Village, New York 11429

Procion^{TM} *dyes*
dye paste activator

Screen Process Supplies Manufacturing Co.
1199 East 12th Street
Oakland, California 94606

vat dyes in paste form

Cloth

Testfabrics, Incorporated
P. O. Box 53
200 Blackford Avenue
Middlesex, New Jersey 08846

cottons, viscose rayons

Nipkow and Kobelt 468 Park Avenue South New York, New York 10016	*silks, by bolt only*
Paron Fabrics 140 West 57th Street New York, New York 10019	*silks, yardage or bolt*

Other suitable fabrics are available locally

Waxes

Paraffin wax: local supermarkets, hardware stores

Mobilwax 2305 (beeswax substitute): check the Order Department of nearest District Office, Mobil Oil Co. for local distributor.

Wax emulsion (cold batik wax):	Durable Arts Company Box 2413 San Raphael, California 94901
Polymer emulsion:	Polyproducts^{TM} Resist 65-512 Polyproducts Corporation 13810 Nelson Avenue Detroit, Michigan 48227

Tjanting tools

Craftools, Inc.
1 Industrial Road
Woodridge, New Jersey 07075

Several dye suppliers also handle tjanting tools

Bibliography

Historical Background

Birrell, Virla. *Textile Arts.* New York: Harper & Brothers, 1959.

Clarke, Leslie. *The Craftsman in Textiles.* Rockville, Maryland: The Unicorn Press, 1968.

D'Harcourt, Raoul. *Textiles of Ancient Peru and Their Techniques.* Seattle: University of Washington Press, 1962.

Glazier, Richard. *Historic Textile Fabrics.* New York: Scribner and Sons, 1923.

Langewis, Laurens. *Decorative Art in Indonesian Textiles.* Amsterdam: C. P. J. Van der Peet, 1964.

Van Stan, Ina. *The Fabrics of Peru.* Leighon-Sea, F. Lewis, 1966.

Weibel, Adele. *Two Thousand Years of Textiles.* New York: Pantheon Books, 1952.

Wheeler, Monroe. *Textiles and Ornaments of India.* New York: Museum of Modern Art, 1964.

Yamanobe, Tomoyuki. *Textiles #2.* Arts & Crafts of Japan, Rutland, Vermont, C. E. Tuttle Company, 1957.

Technical Information

Johnston, Meda and Kaufman, Glen. *Design on Fabric.* New York: Reinhold, 1967.

Keller, Ila. *Batik: The Art and Craft.* Rutland, Vermont: C. R. Tuttle Company, 1966.

Krevitsky, Nik. *Batik: Art and Craft.* New York: Reinhold, 1964.

Lauterburg, Lotti. *Fabric Printing.* New York: Watson-Guptill, 1963.

Maile, Anne. *Tie and Dye as a Present Day Craft.* London: Mills and Boon Ltd., 1963.

Proud, Nora. *Textile Printing and Dying.* New York: Reinhold, 1965.

Russ, S. *Fabric Printing by Hand.* New York: Watson-Guptill, 1966.

Samuel, Evelyn. *Introducing Batik.* Rockville, Maryland: The Unicorn Press.

Tidball, Harriet. *Color and Dyeing.* Lansing, Michigan: Shuttle Craft Guild, 1965.

Film

Batik. ACI Films, Inc., 35 West 45th Street, New York, N. Y. 10036

Acknowledgments

A note of thanks is due to my students, colleagues, and friends who helped in many ways.

The traditional batik cloths, dating prior to World War I, are from the extensive private collection of Mrs. Henry J. Post. Dr. Anna P. Burrell, Harun Arrasjid, and Walter Wells loaned the more recent Javanese and Indian batiks, and the Indian tie dye silks.

The black and white photography is the work of Stephen Mangione, with special help by Paul Pasquerella. Gail Krakauer, Nancy Dayton, and H. Joseph Trapper gave additional assistance in photography.

Several professional textile artists graciously permitted their work to be used: Doris Andrie, Morag Benepe (photographer, Carolyn Fabricant), Marion Bode, Marion Clayden, Ruth Bilowus, and Carter Smith.

Students who kindly allowed their work to be used are: Cynthia Bainbridge, Lauren Belfer, Deanna Donatelli, Carol Edwards, Maribeth Frey, Esther Gaffin, Diane King, Gail Krakauer, Lucille Licata, Peter Sloan, Lee Tetkowski, Neil Tetkowski, Sarah Tobin, Marianne Vallet-Sandre, Gloria Smith, and Nancy Wilford.

(Examples of batik and tie dye work not credited above or by caption are by the author.)

Tie dye panel on satin by the author used as a wall hanging in a room setting. Furniture designed by Wesley Brett.